MW01615054

When
GOD
Says
NO

**Revealing the
YES When Adversity
and Loss Are Present**

Dr. Judith Briles

When God Says NO provides a framework for rethinking the question of your suffering, and for detecting God's presence and purpose (and goodness) in the midst of it.

—John I. Snyder
Pastor | Author, *Your 100 Day Prayer Challenge*

When God Says NO is an incredibly powerful book. I started to read it—I was so floored, so impressed, so MOVED, I couldn't put it down. I've always thought Judith Briles was an amazing woman, but I didn't know half this stuff. Wow! I love the influences of different religions and the personal experiences. I love the sheer optimism. The old proverb "God doesn't give you more than you can carry." She must think Judith is Wonder Woman.

—Rebecca Finkel
graphic designer

Judith is easily the most brilliant, talented, warm-hearted, generous, funny, hard-working, "snappy, sassy, salty" women I've ever had the pleasure of knowing and working with. That she encompasses all of these virtues given her history of horrendous losses, adversity, recovery, and success is a testament to resilience. That she is willing to share so much of her life and how she found peace, strength, and understanding even **When God Says No** is a testament to her love and concern for others. But this book is about more than her personal journey. Filled with Judith's insights as to how she was able to not only survive, but thrive, she shows and tells us how we, too, can overcome even the worst losses by finding a deeper understanding of our faith. I could not put this book down and you are highly likely to find that you can't put it down either until you've finished it.

—Pat Morgan
author, *The Concrete Killing Fields*

Praise for **When God Says NO**

In her deeply moving autobiography, **When God Says NO**, Judith Briles details a life filled with challenges. From a difficult childhood and adolescence to an abusive marriage; to the death of two sons; to betrayal by a business partner who embezzled her money to lies and deceits in the corporate world; to illnesses that brought her to the brink of death; she still triumphed in the end. Throughout this life filled with obstacles; some overwhelming, Judith and her husband John extended help to others also struggling. Her resilience was based on the profound faith that she had a unique purpose and mission in life and in God's plan. It is a spiritual outlook present in all the great religious traditions. Judith's story is a beacon of light and hope in the darkness in an unredeemed, chaotic, low-consciousness world filled with heartbreak, pain and suffering. Judith Briles gets it. She totally GETS it.

—Rabbi Joseph P. Schultz, Ph.D.
In Search of Higher Wisdom:
Conversations About Religion, Spirituality and Mysticism

In her Book, **When God Says NO**, Dr. Judith Briles will take you where you may not want to go, but where so many other believers have suddenly found themselves. She confronts head-on the issue of where God is when unexpected, even shocking, foundation-shaking circumstances have forced upon them the big question, "If God is so good, loving, and faithful, then why did he allow such terrible things to happen to me?"

This is definitely not a book for the faint-hearted, but it is for the broken hearted. Dr. Briles guides the reader through the maze of such "why" questions, and offers us clear hope by showing us how to move beyond the why's, and eventually find God's yes's behind the no's. Nothing theoretical here. No pious platitudes. It's straight out of her own long trek through, and beyond, the Valley of the Shadow of Death.

MileHigh Press

Mile High Press, Ltd.
www.MileHighPress.com
MileHighPress@aol.com
303-885-4460

When God Says NO
Revealing the YES When Adversity and Loss Are Present

Books may be purchased in quantity
by contacting the publisher directly or by calling 303-885-4460.
Mile High Press, Ltd.
8122 South Quatar Circle
Aurora, Colorado 80016

Editing: Peggie Ireland
Cover and Interior Design: Rebecca Finkel, F+P Design

978-1-885331-73-1 hardcover
978-1-885331-76-2 paperback
978-1-885331-74-8 eBook
978-1-885331-75-5 audio

LCCN: 2019934561

Memoir | Inspiration | Grief | Self-Help

Other Books by Judith Briles

How to Create a $1,000,000 Speech

*How to Avoid 101 Book Publishing
Blunders, Bloopers & Boo-Boos*

Snappy Sassy Salty

The Crowdfunding Guide for Authors & Writers

Author and Book Publishing Platforms

AuthorYOU

Show Me About Book Publishing

Stabotage!

Money Smarts for Turbulent Times

Zapping Conflict in the Health Care Workplace

The Briles Report on Women in Health Care

Woman to Woman 2000

The Confidence Factor: Cosmic Gooses Lay Golden Eggs

Woman to Woman

Judith Briles' Money Book

Faith & $avvy, Too!

When God Says No

Stop Stabbing Yourself in the Back

Divorce: The Financial Guide for Women

10 Smart Money Moves for Women

Smart Money Moves for Kids

Money Sense

The Money $ense Guidebook

Raising Money-Wise Kids

GenderTraps

Financial Savvy for Women

The Dollars and Sense of Divorce

Self-Confidence and Peak Performance

The Confident Woman

The Confidence Factor

Money Phases

The Woman's Guide to Financial Savvy

Co-Authored Books

The Tango of Authoring and Publishing

The SeXX Factor

The Dollars and Sense of Divorce

The Workplace

Contents

Author's Note ...

Within *When God Says NO* is a highly personal
journey that starts with the death of my 19-year-
old son Frank. It travels through much of my life, revealing
joy and heartache.

When Frank died, four gifts landed on my doorstep.

The first was the gift of renewal and embracing of the
newness of life, of purpose—it got me in touch with who I
am and what my values are. It taught me how important
my voice was and is; and why it is essential to stand up and
be counted; to reach out, no matter how hurt or angry I feel.

The second was the gift of a renewal of spirituality. It had
taken a backseat in my life for too long ... always there
lingering, but rarely acknowledged on my part.

x When God Says **NO**

The third gift celebrates my "little kid" spirit and keeps it in drive. I was and am willing to work hard … as long as I can find a fun stream within it. Somehow, I will find the humor of a situation.

And the fourth? The fourth gift was one that had carried me from birth. Sometimes subtly; at other times like a roaring wind. Often, not an awareness of it, yet it was there. And a label for it that didn't drop into my consciousness until much later in my living where I could identify it. *The fourth gift was resilience.* It's the gift that keeps on giving … A Yes to the Noes.

Each of these gifts was wrapped from the yeses, the maybes, and the noes that life has and will deliver.

No matter what your faith, there is a Truth within it. Each religion has elements of great goodness, kindness and caring … Be true to it.

I've had enormous success … and enormous failures. But, to me, I have had an amazing life that reminds me of the English gardens that I love—a wide array of flowers, shrubs, and trees; of colors that are dazzling; a whisper that there are surprises within; and a promise of calmness.

Foreword

Have you felt that you didn't know why you were suffering while others seemed to float through life? Have you felt doors closed and there were only noes everywhere you turned? Did you get angry at God as to why He wasn't looking out for you?

This book is a must read for anyone who has had these feelings. If you have experienced severe losses and feel like you can't take another step or just want to feel that someone else understands your story, *When God Says No* is the book for you.

Judith shares her raw journey about the loss of her two children, embezzlement from a business partner, the horrific abuse by her first husband and her near death experience; to connecting with her "Heart Family" … a few of her life challenges that you will discover.

As a great story teller, speaker, writer and mentor to thousands, she brings humor, logic and wisdom for anyone with the desire to heal from almost any crucial loss. Gifted at inspiring people to bring in compassion, forgiveness and tenacity, Judith shares her story with passion, while her execution is to get to the point with insight to healing.

When God Says NO is a powerfully written story of her life that will inspire anyone who feels that life handed them the wrong cards. There were times when she wanted to give up, but as her story unfolds, it reveals how she was able to find the open doors to take the next steps of her life. She found the yeses from the noes, taking her life back … and she shows you how to take your life back when you are dealing with adversity.

I couldn't put *When God Says NO* down. In my profession, I assist thousands to heal from life tragedies. This book will be recommended to my clients for another step in their healing process. It will be life changing for them.

—DEB SHEPPARD
Grief Counselor and Medium
Author, *From Grieving to Believing*

I've Quit School ...

Life is often too long, too hard,
and not fair.

S tanding in front of the bay window in my living room, my youngest daughter Sheryl was perched on my hip. In my view was a group of kids. Among them was Frank, my six-year-old. What he was doing didn't please me. Frank was wolfing down his lunch—his favorite sandwich ... peanut butter and jelly, of course—as he sat on the curb waiting for the school bus. Looking at my watch, it was 8:10 AM.

At his side was his buddy, Robin—matching him bite for bite. Within minutes, the two boys closed their lunch boxes and looked at our front door. Nodding their heads in unison, they stood up, walked across the street, and entered the house. Frank literally slammed his box on the floor while at the same time announcing, "We have quit school. It's too long, too hard and not fair." Shy Robin only nodded his head in agreement.

Sheryl was elated that her brother had returned from the bus stop. At three, she idolized him. Anything that Frank did was okay with her. It wasn't always so with me. Having your six-year-old state that he was dropping out of school was not the ideal way to start my day, or I suspect any mother's day.

Quickly assessing the situation and yes, I was amused at what the two boys had done, I gathered up both lunch boxes and refilled them. As I made a replacement sandwich for each boy, I told them in my best kick-'em-in-the-pants voice, "Life is often too long, too hard, and not fair. Take these sandwiches and march out and wait for your bus. Now!"

Thirteen years later, Frank's six-year-old voice permeated my entire being. Frank was dead. An accident. That Labor Day weekend of 1983 touched thousands of lives. Ten of his friends, including younger sister Sheryl, were with him when he fell twenty feet from the old Dumbarton Bridge into the chilly waters of the San Francisco Bay.

A first for all of them. A tragedy of a close friend … and a sibling. It was a tragedy and heartbreak that would reach out and engulf others—parents, teens and the media in a dominoing spiral that had more twists and turns as it wove its path.

For me, this was not the first time death had touched me so closely. Twelve years earlier, Frank's younger brother Billy had died. An infant. Yet this time, it felt different. It was different.

Every pore in my being shouted out: Life is often too long, too hard and not fair. I wanted off the boat of life.

CHAPTER TWO

There Has Been an Accident ...

I was suspended in death's grip
as life continued around me.

As I finished the dinner dishes, the usual Friday night noises were in the background. We planned to stay in for the evening. A birthday dinner was planned for my husband's birthday with twenty friends the next evening at our home—I was in "prep" mode.

Our life was getting back to normal ... if what we ever did was normal. The two previous years had been hell for me ... a trusted friend and partner had brought in a stealth partner I was clueless about: cocaine. By the time she and her husband were done, they had drained a construction loan that I had personally guaranteed, defrauding me along with several of my clients. By the time the financial storm hit and had drained, I lost in excess of $1,000,000: all our investments; real estate holdings, our home and much of my business. Interestingly, when money isn't as free, even some "friends" were no longer friends. Obviously, they weren't really friends in the first place. Gone were our annual Hawaii vacations and winter skiing. Even my health took a dive when cervical cancer decided it wanted to pay a visit.

I was up to my eyeballs in trying to save the properties. I decided to ease out of my financial firm and sell it within the next two years. Working on my second book, I was transitioning into speaking on a full-time basis as my next career move. Little did I know that the embezzlement I was dealing with would be the stepping stone that would open a new world to me, one that was fulfilling and rewarding. This horrific experience would help me carve out the comeback my family needed and would move us from California to Colorado.

Sixteen and full of herself, Sheryl still had the phone attached to her ear in the family room. The phone was attached to a cord—a phone with only one line that came into our household—and shared by all family members. Mobile phones and "Bluetooth" were still in the future. She was planning the evening's activities as well as the remainder of the long Labor Day weekend ahead with the shared friends she had with her older brother.

Frank was nineteen and still very much a kid—his latest toy was a new kitten, Cashmere. At least we had moved beyond the stage where snakes he had caught in the yard were no longer brought into his room. He had brought her home for Sheryl when her cat had been hit by a car a few weeks earlier. All three of my kids laughed at Cashmere's antics as Frank got her to jump higher and higher, reaching for a bright red ribbon. He worked full-time at a gas station until he could figure out what his next steps were.

Shelley was taking a breather from her school books and just enjoying the end of summer and craziness that always seemed to surround our household. She had been working part-time while carrying a full academic load at college. Saving money, planning for when she would finally have a place of her own, she brainstormed with friends on who would move out first, and declare total independence from the home front. All these items were foremost in her game plan. At twenty-one, Shelley had always been the most responsible of the kids. There were times when I wished she could be as silly as Frank allowed himself to be and, crossing my fingers and toes, as irresponsible as Sheryl had proven to be in the past.

Dishes washed and the phone silent, the kids continued with their plans for the evening. Since it was Daylight Savings Time, they would meet at the drive-in movies for the latest thriller around nine. Frank remarked that he would be in shortly after midnight since he had to open the gas station where he worked at eight the following morning. He would bring Sheryl home with him.

Shelley decided to stay in that night and would meet her friends the next morning.

My husband John arrived home shortly after Frank and Sheryl left with some of their friends who had dropped by. John was extremely busy getting ready for the new year at the college where he taught and served as Chairman of the Science and Engineering Department. With the influx of new students, we rarely saw him before nightfall as each new fall term began.

Relishing the quiet of the evening and making a conscious choice not to do any studying that weekend for the doctorate I was working on, John and I decided to escape with our favorite bowl of popcorn and watch the Friday night movie on TV.

Turning the TV off after the movie and leaving the porch and hallway lights on, we bade good night to Shelley and retreated to our end of the house.

At one in the morning, I awoke suddenly. Something was amiss. I rolled out of bed and wandered

I still felt unsettled. It was 1:10 AM

down the hallway checking on each of the kids. I wondered how many times I had followed in these steps, the steps of the "mommy walk"—the steps that every mother traces when her inner self says "Go."

The check-off began. Shelley was asleep in her room, her door still closed. Sheryl's bedroom door was wide open— I mentally made a note to bean her for being out this late, whatever beaning would mean to me when I saw her in the morning. Frank's door was closed. Remembering his remark that he had to open the gas station at eight in the morning, I knew that getting up early was not on his list of favorite things to do. Assuming he was in bed, asleep, I was relieved he was in. But where was Sheryl?

Letting one of our dogs and two of the cats out, I returned to bed. As I dozed off, my mind told me that it must have been the sound of the animals wanting in and out that had awakened me a few minutes earlier. Otherwise, Frank would have wakened me if there were any problems with Sheryl. Yet something in me didn't agree. I felt something was amiss. It was 1:10 AM.

The clock that hung in our living room struck three times. Sitting straight up, I felt Sheryl's presence at the foot of the bed. Leaping out, I moved toward her, grabbed her wrists and made direct eye contact with her. Without realizing what I was saying, words tumbled out of my mouth. "What do you mean Frank is in the morgue?"

What do you mean Frank is in the morgue?

She was crying and said, "No, Mom, just come," as she took my hand and led me down the hallway that was now brightly lit. John trailed behind me and as our threesome passed Shelley's room, her door opened, and she joined us.

Not knowing where Sheryl was leading our nocturnal train, I found myself in the family room. I first saw the police car through the house windows, and then my eyes met those of the lone policeman standing in the middle of the room.

"Mrs. Briles? I'm sorry. There has been an accident."

My world froze. My mind struggled with the news of Frank's fall. I was suspended in death's grip as life continued around me.

My mind refocused to catch his parting remark: "The Coast Guard will keep searching. I'll call you as soon as there's news."

There was no more sleep as the remainder of the night unfolded. Each of us sat silently with our own tormented thoughts. The radio was turned to the local news station as we hoped, yet feared, to hear some scrap of information.

Automatically, I made pots of coffee and tea and set them on the coffee table. I found a legal pad and pen that could be kept at arm's length ready to jot down any thoughts or news. Shelley and Sheryl were wrapped in blankets at opposite ends of the couch, both losing patience as each hour passed and no mention was made of their brother's fall. Every half hour John checked in with the State Police: "Has the Coast Guard found anything yet?" All believed that just maybe, Frank would be found alive.

Except me. I knew that Frank was gone. When I felt Sheryl at the foot of our bed, I had known it. I had felt it. Unknown to me, my "Mommy walk" was a forewarning. The very same moments I was checking which doors were open and which were closed, Frank had slipped quietly to his death.

As we sat there, between sobs, Sheryl filled in the bits and pieces of what had happened. Everyone had gone to the movies as planned. Bored with the double-bill feature, they left at midnight and convened at the local AM-PM store. The group decided that they would drive out to the old defunct Dumbarton Bridge and climb on it—something that several of them had done in the past for "kicks." With a twelve-pack of beer purchased and adrenaline flowing, ten kids excitedly set out on their daring midnight adventure.

Not all of them climbed. Sheryl stayed down. It was too scary for her. She yelled up to the boys to come down. "Let's go!" She wanted to go home. Gradually each boy descended. Frank was one of the last down. He had climbed before, but his friend Eric was doing it for the first time and was descending above Frank.

As Frank got closer to the bottom of the bridge structure, he stopped and waited for Eric to catch up. He took a step. It was his last. The kids heard a thud, then a splash. They rushed over to the side of the roadway and peered into the bay. A cassette tape from Frank's tape player bobbed on top of the water—the only remaining evidence of his fall.

There was confusion. "What's that?" Night's shadows hid faces. "Who's missing?" Should someone jump in to find out? "It's Frank! He's fallen."

None could believe the nightmare in which they found themselves immersed.

Sheryl ran to one of the cars and jumped in. She fish-tailed, squashing the twelve-pack which lay unopened on the ground, and then straightened the car out and sped to the toll bridge. Surely there would be someone there who could help ... who would know what to do. Who would fix everything?

It seemed to take forever. She reached the tollbooth at 1:12 AM. At first, the operator didn't believe her—he thought she was just a kid up to some kind of prank.

Sheryl persisted. Finally, he got in touch with the State Police who in turn called in the Coast Guard, requesting both boats and helicopters.

Sheryl couldn't conceive that her brother had fallen. That he could be hurt. She was convinced he would be found hanging on to a piling or clinging to a log. Drowning? No longer alive? That wasn't even a possibility to her.

Frank's friends were zombies, almost catatonic. None could believe the nightmare in which they found themselves immersed.

After an hour and a half, the police escorted the kids home. Sheryl lingered at the site—hoping. She was the last to leave, she and the lone policeman.

Back in our living room we waited, dreading the phone call, yet wishing it would come. The police called a few minutes after 6 AM. The Coast Guard had called off their search for the time being. We didn't know what that meant. Later we learned that it meant they had given up. Sheryl tearfully questioned, "I guess there is no hope then?" I wish I could have said yes, that there was always hope. But I couldn't and didn't. There wasn't.

CHAPTER THREE

The Missing Piece ... Why?

My ever-present optimism had disappeared.

I knew when Frank had died. I felt it when I woke in those early hours. It was clear when I suddenly woke when his sister stood at the foot of our bed. In contrast to my clear understanding that he was gone, were the muddled thoughts which fogged my mind. Why did this happen? And to one so young? With so much to look forward to? With so many dreams to realize? Why did this happen to Frank who had finally gotten his act together?

On top of that, as though a chapter had never been completed, all the old aches of Billy's death resurfaced. Billy was my other son—Frank's longed-for baby brother who died in 1971 after living just shy of a week. The impact of each death was so different. Billy's death affected the immediate family and close friends. There had been no services; his ashes were scattered in a rose garden. I couldn't bear to read the cards that were sent from friends, piled away unopened for months.

Acquaintances felt bad and expressed so when our paths crossed ... others would avert their eyes if we happened to come across each other when I ventured out. Mostly, my home was a fortress that I barricaded myself within for months and cared for my three kids. They got fed, dressed and sent to school. During the day, I listened to LPs and painted a scrapbook celebrating the year in the life of a friend that I gave to her on her birthday. It was my therapy. It was all I could manage at the time. And I started to plan my life going forward.

No, this time our family's excruciating loss was in the news. It was public. On the radio. On the TV. Across the newspapers. It was the first death of the long Labor Day weekend. I was visible in the business community. This time there were ten of Frank's friends there when he fell ... and died. This time I couldn't withdraw into a room for three months, painting and listening to records. This time a service had to be held. This

Why ... and why Frank?

time I couldn't escape the nagging questions. And this time I had to have answers.

Why ... and why Frank? This only happens to people in the news. Other people. Yet, this time the airwaves were brimming with reports about *my* family, *my* son, *my* life— a cruel reminder that it was happening to me. Little did I know that such an ordinary Friday night would open a Pandora's box of "Whys?" They became my missing piece. This didn't happen to my close friends ... or to me. Yet it had.

My ever-present optimism had disappeared.

One thing became unmistakably clear. My life had taken a dramatic turn—whether I liked it or not. And with this turn I would never be the same. As days turned into weeks, weeks into months, I found that I could either let myself die with my loss of Frank or discover a new reason to live.

Although no answers came quickly, I searched for hope— not the vain optimism which had kept Sheryl hoping that somehow Frank would be found alive—but another one. *Real* hope. The kind of hope I realized could only be found through a spiritual journey. Somehow, I expected that the bus which arrived at my doorstep when Frank died would take me on. Reluctantly, almost without choice, I boarded that bus.

Why, Why, Why? Our first temptation when confronted with tragedy, any tragedy, is to ask why. John's father, who was undergoing radiation treatments for cancer of the throat, was stunned. Sitting across from me at the breakfast table, he felt it wasn't fair that so young a life was gone. Why not him? He was 86. He had lived a full life. Why not the ones who were already ill? Why a healthy child? A child with promise?

Why Frank?

A therapist friend called. "My entire office is here for you and your family. Our calendars are open at any time." We went. "Feel what you are feeling. Express it: Cry … Anger … Nothing."

She was right—this wasn't a stiff upper lip time. We were in shock. Yet things had to be done. A service had to be planned. Frank's friends were like zombies—roaming from one house to another, in disbelief. All of a sudden, our house was swamped with people.

The phone rang constantly. Each call brought the same questions—how and why?

How could I answer those questions? They were my own questions. I thought of Frank and how his life was taking shape. Finally, he was growing up. He was making plans for the future. He had saved $2,000 to buy the motorcycle of his dreams—papers were to be drawn up Tuesday morning—less than 72 hours after his death. It was the first banking day after Labor Day. I had convinced him to use his savings as collateral for a loan, establishing him as a credit-abiding member of society! He was even cautioning his younger friends that it was stupid to drop out of high school—they needed to continue with their education.

Frank had taken a lot of years to arrive at this newfound maturity, taking plenty of side roads along the way. We had removed him from the house twice in his brief life. The first came when he got involved with a group of kids whose influence was negative with a capital "N." A new school, boarding away for six months, finally broke the spell. He need to break away from the "old crowd." Years later, when we experienced similar problems with his younger sister, he suggested that we do the same with her. He had said he hated me then, but he thanked me as he looked back. Whew—it was heady stuff for a parent finally to hear her actions validated.

The second time was when he was eighteen. We had a rule that if graduation had occurred, then each kid could stay in the house rent-free if he or she was going to college full time. Otherwise, rent had to be paid and a full-time job obtained … or move out. Frank didn't believe me. Well, not at first. He thought we were kidding. We weren't. We changed the locks, put his clothes in his truck and let him know that he was not welcome. This happened only after we gave repeated warnings that D-Day was approaching. He threatened to sleep on the front lawn—what would the neighbors think? I told him I didn't care what they thought. I made his favorite dinner—the last supper. And I had told him that this was it … he was on his own after this last meal. He laughed. Then he got mad. He grasped that I wasn't bluffing. Mom was serious.

Frank slept in his truck for three nights, then moved in with a friend. The friend's mother called and I explained the circumstances; what our rule was; and suggested that she charge rent if he was going to stay there. Frank wasn't welcome at our house unless he was going to school or worked and paid rent.

Within ten days, he called my office and made an appointment with my secretary to see me. Arriving, he said, "I have a job ... can I move back and rejoin our family?"

"I ... we ... want you back ... but there are a few conditions ..."

Frank and I created a contract that contained duties, rights, privileges, along with paying his share based on his new and independent income. He revealed he wasn't ready to go to college and needed a year off from school. He still wanted to *be home* with all of us. Amazingly, Frank was talking as an emerging adult to me. He was on his way to becoming a responsible, productive adult. And back he came.

So why now? Why did this happen when Frank had begun to make positive choices in his life? Why didn't God prevent the accident from happening? It wasn't as if Frank was a bad kid. We weren't perfect, but we were good people—people who had lived by the Golden Rule. We taught our kids about right and wrong. We taught them to help others in need—I can't count how many times we had extra kids in our home that ours had brought in like stray dogs—they needed a place to stay … there were problems at home. We taught them about being responsible with money starting at an early age. We taught them that if they were to "get" … then they would have to "give."

Other people got their miracles. Why didn't we?

In reality, life is often simply not fair.

Even as I asked these questions, I began to understand that *Why me* question; Why was a two-sided question. On the other side of the coin was the stark question, *Why not me?* It's not as though I deserved a corner on good luck. Look around you. Tragedy strikes without warning, and often without any relationship to a person's moral character. What a person does or does not contribute to society is irrelevant. Parents lose their children every year through accidents. Awful things happen through-out every day—awful things that have no rationale or reason to them.

In reality, life is often simply not fair.

The question then becomes, *Why isn't life fair?*

> If God could prevent these things from happening, is there a cruel and sadistic undercurrent?
>
> Does God find some kind of perverse pleasure in our suffering?
>
> Is God a master game player?
>
> If God can't prevent these things from happening, then what's this about the claim to being all-powerful?
>
> Just what makes God tick?

Some would try to ennoble our suffering by saying that God is trying to "teach us a lesson" or that we are somehow "special" because He has "chosen" us to suffer a certain fate. I have heard these phrases more times than I care to count. Being taught a lesson or being special or chosen to be the recipient of bum luck, or a tragedy, is alien to me. All were unsatisfactory answers.

As Frank's mother, I certainly understood that I sometimes had to choose an unpopular means of discipline. After all, I did boot him out of the house after he graduated from high school and he chose to loaf. That was thirty-plus years ago. Would I do the same thing today … where kids routinely are dependent on their parents well into their twenties? Yes. Yes, I would. But it was a lesson in "tough love" that was for his benefit. I felt, and still feel, that parents should be parenting first rather than be a "pal."

The punishment was appropriate. His blasé attitude led to the ignoring of our house rules. He was aware of the consequence if he chose to ignore the path he needed to be on to become an adult.

In this instance, there was no crime to relate to Frank's death. It was arbitrary. Somehow, I couldn't believe in an arbitrary God who would let my son die or allow my child to be killed—to teach him or me or my family a lesson. What would the lesson have been?

> *You shouldn't have stayed out so late.*
>
> *You should have been more careful not to lose your footing.*
>
> *You should have been a better mother and then Frank would have known better than to go climbing out on a dangerous bridge.*

On the other hand, if being "chosen" by God to suffer the death of both my sons was an answer to my *whys*—then to my way of thinking, there are plenty of other candidates out there. Let Him choose someone else. Not me. Not us. I'd rather have Frank and Billy here than to be writing a book about my struggles to find purpose in my pain.

No, the God of love and compassion I had been taught about was someone who could part the sea; who healed the sick; and who forgave the sinful. Not one who created pain. I, like other parents, struggled to grasp why this was allowed to have happened.

The passage of Deuteronomy 29:29 shares: "There are secrets which the Lord your God has not revealed to us, but these words which he has revealed are for us and our children to obey forever." And Jeremiah 29:11-14 reveals: "For I know the plans I have for you, says the Lord. They are plans for good and not for evil, to give you a future and a hope. In those days when you pray, I will listen. You will find me when you seek me, if you look for me in earnest. Yes, says the Lord, I will be found by you."

My take is that God doesn't want us to experience evil things. That there is hope and a future. But, it's a two-way street—reach out. He is there.

As a child, having secrets with my friends was grand fun. It wasn't now. My rational adult side tells me that there are things we may never understand in life—things where the answers just don't bubble up with a snap of the fingers. Things that remain a mystery and at times, even a miracle. Secret things. But when you hurt, sometimes the rationale takes a back seat.

Soon, I began to understand *that focusing on the why* would prevent me from ever moving on to my place of peace. In a real sense, there was no answer to my *whys*. When asking, the clouds gathered to obstruct the past, the present, and the future. It was easy for the *why* to join with its paralyzing mate, *if only*. You, me, everyone has had the *if only* circulate in thoughts and conversations. *If only* creates a haunting dance around misfortune, hurts, loneliness, fear, and sickness.

When you flip the coin, the question becomes, *Why not me?* Inclusion enables you to move forward to experience and explore the future rather than being plagued, obsessed, and embittered by the past.

My future was unalterably changed by Frank's death. My experiences, feelings and thoughts were and are different from the ones when Billy died. My thoughts, my passions, my lifestyle will not be what they were before Frank's tragic fate. But now I know that I no longer feel the need to ask why. Not because it's wrong to ask, but because I've grown beyond that question. And growing beyond means I'm not stuck in the past.

For me, *why* was the window to a deeper and richer understanding of life. *Why* was the question that helped me to begin to understand the *noes*, but more importantly, the *yeses*. Letting go of *why* opened up fantastic doors—doors that I never knew existed. These doors have allowed me to look back at my past experiences—the good times and the bad—and be able to say, "I have a good life. I have a rich life." Would I want to experience many of the heartaches and mishaps that have gotten me to where I am? No. Yet, I have a good life and a rich one.

CHAPTER FOUR

Noes Lead to Yeses

*I went home empty-handed,
empty-hearted. So alone.*

My babies always came early, from four to six weeks early. Sheryl, my third, had a mind of her own when she was going to show up. She still does today. We barely made it to the hospital. My husband dropped me off and I was whisked to a room where I climbed into a bed. Within minutes and with no help, Sheryl debuted—just she and I in that small room. I felt better. A nurse popped in the door with an, "Oh-oh … she's already delivered."

This is baby number four. At seven weeks before my due date, I'm at my OB's for a routine check—an OB that many of my friends had said was the best. "You've dropped," he tells me. "I know—the baby will be here any day now," I say.

His amusement is on his face. I continue, "All my finger-nails have broken—it's the sign that tells me my baby will come at any time." He laughs and shakes his head. "You have many weeks to go …"

"No, it will be soon. My body is saying it's about done. It's the same way it has been my other three times …"

Two days later, my time had come with the familiar belly and backaches. My doctor was off, and his backup was there. Everything feels wrong. What's wrong? What's taking so long? Labor was so quick with each of my babies. All I could think was, Help! Don't let something be wrong with my baby. I never used drugs with my deliveries and I'm at the end of the pain rope. I can't stand it any longer. Breathe. Breathe, I tell myself. The baby will be okay. Breathe. I want this baby out. One more push.

I hear a nurse say, "He's here. It's a boy!"

A boy, I smile! There are ten fingers. Ten toes. He's even got hair! Oh my—a first! It was so exciting! Six pounds, seven ounces. He's crying. He sounds great. The nurses check reflexes and breathing. Perfect score: ten. He's perfect—my fourth perfect baby! But something's still wrong, with me.

I sense it, I knew it as the afterbirth wouldn't deliver; I couldn't push it out. I was so tired … but at least my baby was okay. He was okay, right?

Billy wasn't okay. Within the week, he died. He was premature—six weeks early. His was such a short life. His lungs just weren't ready: Hyaline-Membrane disease. Because his weight was so normal and his test scores came out so good, the doctors and nurses didn't recognize the danger he was in. They thought I was wrong—he was not premature. Yes. Yes, he was.

As his lungs collapsed, Billy gasped for his last breath and died in the middle of the night. It was all so unnecessary because of ignorance. So preventable with medication. So unfair. Yet for whatever reason, God allowed it. He could have said yes, but for some mysterious reason, He said no. I was upset. It didn't help when the hospital staff wouldn't let me hold or even see my baby. It didn't help when they never told me what to do or what was happening.

I knew they were coming for me.

My roommate was a woman who didn't want another baby. Hers was brought into our room for feeding; mine remained in the nursery. Times were medieval in thinking in the 1970s—mothers holding and touching babies in trouble just wasn't done. When I heard the footsteps coming toward my room late at night, I knew they were coming for me. Wheeling my bed out of the room—all I heard was: "We are sorry about your baby … but you are no longer a new mother … we have to take you out of maternity to the general medical floor."

What? What? I was in shock … and I wanted to escape. When I was left alone, I got up. Found some clothes … headed to the lobby, called a cab and walked out of that hospital. Never to return to it … or the medical team who was supposed to be there for me and for my son. My body, my mind, my heart, my soul—all were prepared to nurse and nurture and love this little boy. How do you deal with a body that is prepared for a baby when there is no baby? No one told me.

I went home empty-handed, empty-hearted. So alone.

The kids were elated to discover I was home early in the morning. Shelley, Frank and Sheryl all came running to see their baby brother. Their father hadn't told them that he had died. It was another task for my empty heart to deal with. There was no baby brother to show them.

I was furious with the doctor and angry with the hospital. My doctor called me and asked me to come in when I felt better. He reminded me that I shouldn't have sex for six weeks. What is wrong with this picture? I never wanted to set foot in that hospital or see that doctor again. But I didn't feel anger toward God. Somehow, that didn't hit me as an option. It's just that this nagging question of *Why* kept coming up. Why did my baby have to die? Why weren't my prayers answered? Why did God say no? My perfect, innocent baby boy.

Deep in my heart, I buried my questions. That is, until Frank's death. But when Frank died, I needed to know that there was some reason for all the pain, all the tragedy that was circling. Certainly, others had suffered more, but somehow, I didn't believe I deserved all this. Somehow, I didn't believe a good and loving God could overlook the tragedies in our lives and be unaffected. Uncaring. Or worse yet, unwilling to stop it.

The anguish I felt was no different than the pain shared by any parent, including biblical parents. In the Old Testament, the poignant and familiar story of David appears. After taking Bathsheba and having her husband killed, David pleads with God to save his baby. The baby didn't sin. David fasts and prays. He repents and humbles himself before God. Yet this innocent life, this precious baby ... dies. God said no. Quietly, decisively, inexplicably, no.

Noes Lead to Yeses

It was this way until I discovered a mysterious truth. That behind every no lurks a yes. And that yes is woven into the fabric of a plan that reaches far beyond our own lives.

The truth unfolded one Sunday morning as I sat in the sanctuary full of much-pained people in the summer of 1985. The church I was a member of had been driven apart by a series of events involving the senior pastor—a man who had been there for me ... and all the kids when Frank died. He had become someone that I barely recognized ... a man on the path of self-destruction. He had become an alien as the fellowship was ripped apart.

Members were pitted against members. Personal and financial information was bandied about by the congregation. As Stewardship Chair, I was sickened to learn that records I felt such a responsibility for were leaked to others. I was pained by the depths of anger, fear, hostility—even hatred—that permeated the air.

Where was God? He couldn't possibly be here, not with us. Yet He was. The day before, a special meeting of the congregation had been called. We had just finished an intensive multi-week counseling/evaluation by a group that specializes in conflicts within the church. This was an understatement, to say the least, with what had been going on. The results were to be presented to all. The night before, our Session had met with both pastors and members from the Presbytery. Resignations were requested, submitted, and accepted.

You are needed ... you need to be there.

The past several months had been grueling. I couldn't imagine what had been in my mind when I accepted the nomination to the Session of our church. There I found myself an elected elder, hated by a group within the church, party to information that was privileged and could not be exposed. My mind played gymnastics; if only they knew the truth.

For months, I had a dialogue with God. Why was I here? Why, when I was in the midst of such personal turmoil? Why, when my wounds from Frank's death were so open, so raw? The answer was always the same, "You are needed ... you need to be there."

During this period, I can remember driving home from the airport hating the position I was in—seeing "friends" I cared for destroy their friendships as they were pitted against each other. But the internal dialogue continued: You need to be there. I wanted to resign as several of the other elders had done. I wanted out. I was being pulled apart by people I cared for. I felt as I had when Frank died—so vulnerable, so alone, so hurt.

My inner voice continued: *I need you there.* Stay. Tears streamed down my face as I drove. But I made the commitment to hang in there—hatred, pain and all. Who was dropping these words in my head?

On that Sunday, an amazing thing happened. An Associate Pastor had been sent to fill the void. He was to lead our services and communion. It became a good day for me. The title of his sermon became the title of this book: "When God Says No." Words were put to my anguish. That

sermon changed my life and those of hundreds of others.
For the first time, an incredible feeling of peace descended
from the rafters, enveloping all who sat there that morning.
God—through Dr. John Snyder—stayed with our congregation for more than a year. He brought the depth of his
knowledge, caring, spirituality, and healing skills to our
small town in Northern California. It was a miracle for me
... for so many. Through his sermons I began to discover
the yeses behind God's noes.

As every parent knows, raising a child can be an incredible
challenge. One illustration John Snyder used was so simple,
and so logical—that of a mother telling her child no. No
caring mother would knowingly want her child in an unsafe
or potentially dangerous situation. Rather, she says no. No
pleading, begging or tantrums can change her mind. Behind
the no is a yes ... yes as in, "I don't want you to hurt yourself. I care for you. I love you."

In turn, when God gave the Israelites the law, He conveyed
it with a yes behind His stern no. "And now, Israel, what
does the LORD your God require of you, but to fear the
LORD your God, to walk in all his ways, to love him, to
serve the LORD your God with all your heart and with all

your soul, and to keep the commandments and statutes of the LORD, which I command you this day for your good?" Deuteronomy 10:12-13.

There was a list of rules. Not rules for the sake of rules, nor to be harsh. Rather, they were rules that would be filled with benefits.

Through John Snyder's explanations of these truths, I was able to move forward through the bitter struggles of our church to a deeper understanding of life's noes. All my questions weren't answered and all my whys weren't put to rest, but I was able to begin putting the puzzle back together despite the missing pieces. When John accepted a position with another church, his work was done. He had been able to heal several immense wounds.

He brought phenomenal wisdom with his sermons, his insights. The Reverend Dr. John Snyder has been one of God's miracles for me … as well as for so many others. It wasn't a goodbye—I knew that he wasn't gone from my life and that we would stay in contact. I just knew. I loved his latest book, *Resenting God*, and was honored to endorse it.

Years later, Rabbi Joseph Schultz crossed my path. Referred by another client, he wanted to publish his final book, *The Kabbalistic Journey.* I confess, I knew nothing about the Kabbalah until he came to my offices for help in finalizing it and getting it published. I always write the back covers for my clients and for a solid week, I carried Joe's manuscript up and down the stairs of my home. Then the words flowed to complete our work.

When he first sat down at my conference table, I thought "Yoda" had arrived. The wisdom and presence permeated from him to me. After three days of work, he headed back to his home in Boston. Before he left, I gave him a copy of William Campbell's *The Power of Myth.* Asking him to look it over; to read it … I said, "This has you written all over it. I know you are tired; I know that you think The Kabbalistic Journey is your last book … but I don't think it is. There is one more. I want you to consider sitting down with someone you trust. Someone who understands the Kabbalah. And someone who will ask you open-ended questions and record your answers. Out of that send-off came *Conversations of a Higher Wisdom*—a book that we all agree is the best yet!

Both these individuals—Reverend John Snyder and Rabbi Joseph Schultz—came into my life at the right time and for the best of all reasons. We all stay in contact—both are "reality checks" with the world for me … and I for them.

A smile always crosses my face when I think of them. Yeses are present.

CHAPTER FIVE

No ... Yes ... Not Yet

There are times when what happens,
happens for a greater good.

Present day, you can't turn on the radio, watch TV, or read a newspaper in print or online without a bombardment of bad news. Natural disasters shout out: earthquakes, tornadoes, hurricanes, typhoons, floods, drought, and fire (natural and man-induced). Environmental challenges and climate change add to the mix. Then there are human-incited disasters—from war, murder, kidnappings, opioid addiction, betrayal, riots, violence, and scandals. Sometimes the list seems endless. When it comes to human activities, mayhem fills the bill.

You and I are interconnected globally with other countries and peoples. You and I are part of a larger picture—a larger plan. You and I are part of a continuum. If you believe as I do, then the events in our lives have greater significance than our immediate sojourn here on earth. There is a vantage point and perspective that you and I don't have. We may not see anything positive being created from bad news, pain, and suffering. Hindsight, however, allows us to see that there are times when what happens, happens for a greater good.

Don't get me wrong. I'm not suggesting we are "pawns" in the "game" of life. Neither am I suggesting that some greater good justifies evil or that God is the culprit of all things going bad. What I am proposing is that there may be instances when what is perceived as an immediate evil can work for a greater good. I'm also saying that what happens in our lives is significant—beyond the scope of our own lives. Behind every *no* lies a *yes*. What it means is this: In the overall fabric and plan of God, He hasn't lost control.

We were in it together ... this grieving and healing process. All of us.

The Power of Prayer

If each of us lives to be 80, we will share 29,200 days earthbound. I can't pretend to understand all the purposes of God, but I do know we are all inextricably bound together in this mass known as humanity. Somewhere, in all the *noes* of life, there is a *yes* to be discovered. It is not just a romantic ideal that obliterates and disguises pain. It is a truly powerful, authoritative and life-giving *yes*.

Out of Billy's death emerged a beautiful tapestry of life. I didn't see it at first. Nor did I expect anything positive to surface. I hurt too much. Yet, through his death, I learned to truly value the lives of little children.

Through his death, I learned to value my children, the healthy children whom I took for granted.

Through his death, I learned that the dust will be there tomorrow, so go play with my kids today.

Through his death, I learned how not to be victimized by hospital staff, and others who tell you what you can or can't do.

Through his death, courage entered my life and I took steps to get out of an abusive marriage.

Through his death, my compassion for others grew.

And through his death, I discovered this simple prayer that was brought to me on a small medal by a close friend:

> *God grant me the serenity to accept the things I cannot change,*
>
> *to change the things I can,*
>
> *and the courage and wisdom to know the difference.*

It has become one of my mainstays—I recited it daily. They were small steps that I took back then in 1971. Baby steps. Since then, each step has brought me closer to a realization of the way in which God works in our lives. That prayer, famous for its use with alcoholics, became my stepping stone to a greater understanding of God's role in my life and my role in prayer.

Prayer is something most struggle with. Anyone who has ever prayed an "unanswered prayer" knows the frustration, and the disappointment, of feeling that his or her outreach for help hasn't been heard.

It seems very simplistic to say that God simply answers some of our prayers with a "no." In fact, it sounds as if we're making excuses. It sounds like a pat answer to avoid the real question of unanswered prayer. Often it sounds as if we're doing theological gymnastics to protect our faith or the faith of someone we care about.

I know that if others hadn't reached out to me when Frank died, my days would have seemed endless. I, in turn, reached out to his ten friends to help them process their grief, that in their disbelief, their sudden awareness that they weren't the invincible lot they thought themselves to be. In fact, that most young people assume to be … invincible.

We were in it together … this grieving and healing process. All of us.

I know that I had my alone times and down times. Mine were filled with self-talk and quiet prayer. And with my own time alone, I discovered early on, I wasn't alone. Externally, I felt myself enveloped with a layer of concern—as though someone had literally taken me in his or her arms. Someone was loving me, stroking me, telling me that I was safe. I was. Somehow, I was being lifted and nurtured. Where was that coming from?

The question is, then, why does God say "no" to healing a mother with little children from her cancer? Why would God withhold an answer to save my baby from dying? Why would God allow children in the war-torn Middle East to lose arms and legs in a cruel war? It's a huge "why."

The Glass Towers

I was in Boston a few years ago, sitting on a bench near the Freedom Trail. It was a rest break. My eldest daughter and I had been walking, shopping, and sightseeing since early morning. As I took in my surroundings, I got up and was pulled toward some type of structure. Not knowing what it was, I sensed that it was powerful, and I should be there. That I should explore it. As I approached the first of six glass-like structures, I crossed a grate—a grate that suddenly released whiffs of warm air. *How odd*, I thought. Standing within one of the structures, I see rows and rows of numbers. Moving from structure to structure, just looking, I get it … and I back up, and call to my daughter. "You need to see this … experience this."

Back we go; now exploring and reading everything. We are in the middle of the New England Holocaust Memorial. *Stunning* was my immediate reaction. The glass-like tall structure is indeed glass. The numbers I noticed are white and one million of them wrap around the interior of each from the floor to the many-storied top. Six million numbers. Each of these towers represents one of the six death camps, a reminder of the six million Jews killed during the Holocaust and the six years of World War II. The numbers represented the registration numbers of the victims.

I love quotes and notice that they are scattered throughout and they become a magnet, pulling me in and along. One reads:

> *Most infants and children were killed immediately upon arrival at the camps. The Nazis murdered as many as one and a half million Jewish children.*

Strategically placed after the last tower is one that I have seen many times. One that I have referenced countless times when I'm confronted with ignorance ... and when people choose not to speak up to injustices and wrong-doing. Stopping and looking back at the towers, I read, and reread it:

They came first for the Communists,
and I didn't speak up because I wasn't a Communist.

Then they came for the Jews,
and I didn't speak up because I wasn't a Jew.

Then they came for the trade unionists,
and I didn't speak up because I wasn't a trade unionist.

Then they came for the Catholics,
and I didn't speak up because I was a Protestant.

Then they came for me,
and by that time no one was left to speak up.

—Martin Niemoeller

Why did God allow six million Jews to be annihilated in the Holocaust? And, why has God said no to me … and to you … and to others?

Speaking up. Speaking out. They are gifts. Do you use them? Do you have reminders to nudge yourself to "not forget" …? I do. Years ago, I kissed my 50th birthday. I was having dinner with several of my friends in San Francisco. Nicole showed up with a large brown, butcher-paper-wrapped gift. As I unwrapped it, all of us were mesmerized by what she shared. "My mother and I wanted to give you something special. We both know that you love flowers, and this is something she wanted you to have."

What is revealed is an oil painting. A still life of a bowl of flowers framed in an old gold-colored frame. I know that I have a "treasure" in my hands.

Nicole continues. "This was one of the paintings the Nazis took from us, when my parents were taken. You can find out who the artist is by having the blacked-out section removed."

"Removed?" I questioned.

"It was common for the Nazis to paint over the name of the artist and add another."

Sure enough, in the lower corner, I see a dark swatch of paint that doesn't quite match the true background. On the opposite corner, a name is painted in—*Wren*.

The gift overwhelms me. I love it. Yes, the garden and flowers are one of my things ... but the survival and thrival story that Nicole Shapiro and her family carry is what movies salivate over. It's a story I know well from decades of friendship. Nicole's father was murdered in the camp. Her mother survived. A nun had taken Nicole in and protected her as an infant in a convent. It was several years before mother and daughter were reunited. When the nuns told young Nicole her mother had come, Nicole said, "Mary?" thinking that the only name connected with "mother" was Mary from her many years in the convent.

And now, to have a connection to my friend in my home is an amazing concept to me. I've chosen to not find out who the real artist is. Hanging in the entryway of my home, I wanted to be reminded of what bigotry and hatred did and is. And routinely, I share the "rest of the story" with visitors to my home. I have no idea of the monetary value, if there is one. What I know is that it is priceless to me.

Misconceptions

Part of the problem is the belief that bad things should happen only to bad people. In his pivotal bestseller, *When Bad Things Happen to Good People,* Harold S. Kushner points out that somewhere deep inside people is the belief that if something bad happens to someone, then there must be a reason. One of the first responses we have is, "What did I do to deserve this?" Surely, I could have done nothing so "bad" that the life of my baby and my child would be taken.

There's a belief in a direct cause and effect. This is reinforced in our childhood; we are punished for bad behavior and rewarded for good behavior. In the same way, we believe that the things which happen to us here on

How unjust. How unfair. How like life.

earth have a direct relationship to our behavior. If we are *good*, then God will reward us. If we are *bad*, then God will punish us.

That all seems so logical. So down to earth. So full of common sense. But is it? If you are "good," is that a guarantee that everything will go well for you? I don't think so. There are too many people out there whom I have had to work with and around that I would classify as "bad" ... at times even downright evil. And yet, life's breaks come their way— the decision-makers, the people in charge, don't see the bad sides. The "bad" keep getting rewarded. How unjust. How unfair. How like life.

We all have tapes like these running through our minds. And one of those tapes is that bad things only happen to bad people. Never us. Only them. And good things/

blessings happen only to "good" people. Us, you, me—not "them." Right?

The Jews of the Old Testament saw it that way as well. Whenever there was a time of prosperity, *everyone* said, "God is blessing us." If there was a famine, *everyone* said, "God is punishing us." The Book of Job is a classic illustration of this type of mindset.

Job's family died, he lost his fortune, and he was stricken with boils. Everyone, including his wife, said, "God is doing this to you." Job thought so, too. His wife's response was, "Why don't you just curse God and die? After all, it was God's fault that these disasters are happening to you."

Job's wife wasn't alone in her response. Her reaction bubbled up in Greek thought as well. In Greek mythology, the common belief was that the gods were up in heaven making it hard for humans on earth. They were sitting around thinking up "divine dirty tricks" that they could play on people. Some of that same philosophy is still around today. At times, the humans would make offerings to the gods, to get on the "good side." Sometimes it worked; most times it didn't.

Often, this is how we are, too. We become angry when God doesn't accept our "good offer"…"If You heal my child, I'll do anything You want; if You get me out of this mess, I promise I'll never do it again." Famous last words. Based on our own sincerity, we believe that God should say *"yes."* But for reasons we can't always understand, God says *"no."* He doesn't heal our child; He doesn't get us out of the mess we created. So, we become angry. It doesn't work. We retaliate by being less kind to others. Rarely does that pay off.

The reality is: anger needs to be directed where it belongs.

When Frank died, I was initially angry with the situation. It was an accident. It could have been any one of those kids climbing on the bridge who fell. It just happened to be my Frank. Did God stop it? *No.* Could God have prevented it? *Yes.* Did it break God's heart? *I believe so.* But God chose not to intervene. God not only gave us the freedom to be right, He gave us the freedom to be wrong. And that freedom extends to all of life, to all of creation. In the context of that freedom, God chooses at times not to intervene. God doesn't always say *no.* Sometimes, it is a *not yet.*

CHAPTER SIX

I Was Lost ... and Stuck

When your internal dialogue has built up, it becomes a mountain, and I couldn't quite get over that mountain.

Never in my life had I been pushed down like this. This time, I was stuck. Really, truly stuck. And it wasn't just in a small way. I was so lost, I couldn't even make a phone call. At least, after Frank's death, I was able to go through the mechanics. Certain rituals were expected of me. A service had to be planned. As soon as morning dawned, I had begun making calls to all the people involved. I called Frank's place of work; I tracked down family. And I phoned our friends to tell them that John's birthday dinner slated for the evening was canceled. Each and every call was painful. All those questions that my calls generated compounded our hurts, pains, and fears. And then I waited for the dreaded phone call from the searchers.

But this time, I was paralyzed. For someone on the outside looking in, being misled and cheated in a business venture may seem trivial in comparison to the loss of my two children, but somehow, this was my catastrophic event—my breaking point.

In living color, my work, a creative project that I had spent years developing, was being destroyed before my very eyes. Another child was dying. Worse yet, I couldn't believe that the death blows were delivered by someone I had trusted, respected, even defended. It was more than I could bear to realize

I had learned to develop a great façade—to pretend when things were not going well.

that I had been lied to by representatives of the company. I believed that contracts had been altered after my signature had been obtained. Promised reimbursements of expenses amounting to many thousands of dollars were brushed aside. To me, everything was done to destroy my project—my baby. The personal devastation was so total that I couldn't make a simple phone call. I couldn't work; I was paralyzed. I didn't think I could even live. I was a mess!

In the public eye as a professional speaker, I had learned to develop a great façade—to pretend when things were not going well. There was never the luxury of shutting down. The show must go on! This time, though, it was different.

I panicked. I had enormous financial obligations and every penny of the money due from the grant had been budgeted and planned for—a great deal of it already spent. When my work and my efforts were sabotaged, one of my "babies" was being harmed, and my very being cried out in pain.

My legal counsel assured me that my case was strong. My agent said that the company would support and testify if I pursued the legal route. The evidence appeared to be clearly in my favor. But was it? How can you measure years of work outside of the hard dollars spent? I was convinced that I was legally right. But my years of experience in the business world had shown me that just about anyone can be right in a legal situation, and still lose. That, in fact, the attorneys became the overall winners in the end. For some, legalese becomes the solution. For me, it wasn't.

I couldn't face another *no*.

When your internal dialogue has built up, it becomes a mountain, and I couldn't quite get over that mountain. You see, the real issue was, I just couldn't take a third death. Weren't two children enough? I had carried that project not just for nine months, but for several years. I had lived with it, defended it, supported it, nurtured it and given birth to it—just to have it snatched away from me.

Not Another No

I couldn't face another *no*. This time I was broken, openly broken. For the first time in my life, there was no fight left in me. There were no inner reservoirs of strength. No *yeses* behind the unexplained *no*. I was stuck in that gray, mournful area of the *no that leads to nowhere*. I had entered what I now term the "being-stuck syndrome." And I couldn't get out by myself.

Desperate, I needed help. I wanted—no, I needed—to end my pain, my hurt, the betrayal I felt so deeply. I had kids to take care of. I had clients who wanted my advice, and it was like I had duct tape across my mouth. I couldn't talk to anyone close to me without tears in my eyes. After all I had gone through, this was the first time I had felt that life was not worth living. I was ready to throw in the towel.

Bucking Up Isn't the Answer

I called my friend and former pastor, John Snyder. We all need a John Snyder in our lives, and I was very blessed to have him in mine. I couldn't talk without tears. He listened patiently, then spoke words that I'll always be grateful for. He didn't tell me to "buck up." He didn't ask me just to forget it and move on. He listened, then he expressed his own outrage: "This really makes me angry." Oh, how I needed that understanding and support!

He saw the injustice. There was no attempted cover-up, no "Christian blackmail" telling me my feelings were invalid and if I were truly the person I should be, I would feel forgiveness toward the malicious perpetrator of the crime. It was okay to cry. It was okay to be human. It was okay to feel lost and hopeless and despairing of life itself. He helped me to process my feelings internally. I had a partner in pain who was there for me. I could spill it all out!

John Snyder was the first step. The second was a little harder for me. I had always been so independent ... so self-assured ... so together. At least, that's what everyone had always thought. This time the "I-can-do-it-myself syndrome" was broken. I couldn't do it by myself. I couldn't do anything for myself, much less anyone else. I had to reach out to friends. To family. That was a big step for me. Everyone had always counted on me, the pillar. And you know what? They were there.

Reaching Out

When I called, I asked for their thoughts, their strategies, but most of all, I asked for their prayers and stream of conscious thoughts, good thoughts, to be directed my way. Help came freely, with love and concern. "How much money do you need to get over the hurdle?" asked Carol as we sat down to a glass of iced tea. Carol had been my business partner before we had parted ways and went on different paths. My friend Marilyn called for a catch-up call and to say hello—did she get an earful! The following day a check for several thousand dollars was delivered to my home with a note, "I love you! I know that God has plans for you."

That note and check broke me out. I am loved. "You are a valuable person," was what I heard and felt. Another person cares for me. Marilyn and other friends Susan, Coreen, Joyce, and Nicole routinely checked in with me—

reminding me that I was loved, my voice was important. They kept me uppermost in their prayers.

One Saturday I poured out my heart to a group of speakers within The National Speakers Association of Northern California. We called ourselves "The Masters." They were stunned. This was show-and-tell time for the big shots. This was when we got to brag, to share good news from the

> **What do you mean you have *garbage* going on in your life?**

previous month or ideas that we picked up that could be used. Everyone in the group was always doing great. We were the ones on the top. We were the ones on stage. Our stories were always terrific. We always looked great. We made money—some of us, a lot. Successful.

"What do you mean you have *garbage* going on in your life?" echoed around the room.

Yet here I was, immersed in a giant trash heap. The sharp business woman had been shafted, really shafted.

After that Saturday, several notes came in from some of the speakers in the group thanking me for opening up, for giving "permission" to reveal ... and ask for help. Ironically, a few in that high-powered group shared that they were going through rough times as well. And of course, me being me, I started brainstorming with them … to help. "What can I do for you … maybe there's something we can do together to fuel us both … I've got a client that I think needs your wisdom … ." The sounding board of support had surfaced.

I had reminded them that life's not always a merry-go-round. In getting out of the "being-stuck syndrome," I had been forced to reach out. And in reaching out, I touched other lives. Sharing my hurt gave permission for others to admit that sometimes all was not great. Their caring, their friendship, and their prayers became my food. I was beginning to take in the nutrition I needed.

As long as I had been wallowing in my anger, in my rage at being taken, I was stuck. Going nowhere. But when I began to look outward, to reach out my hand to others, something magical, mystical, began to happen—that special something that happens when one life touches yours and your life touches another. I was no longer fighting a private war. I had friends and allies to see me through.

Forward

Looking back, what my friends reminded me of were my accomplishments. I was so devastated, so broken, so bereft of self-esteem, that I had forgotten what I *had* done. Here I had spent several years on what I thought was one of my best and most creative projects to date, and my confidence had been shattered via the nonsupport of a group I had trusted.

Ironically, as I was experiencing this tremendous pain, I had committed to writing a book on confidence for a publisher for whom I had written a book the previous year. Crazy, right? Here I was doing a survey on confidence, writing a book on confidence ... and I was struggling to find my own! What a sense of humor God has—or was it something else? Would this something else add strength to the surgery on my life that I was experiencing?

Out of the hundreds of women interviewed and thousands surveyed for the book, *The Confidence Factor,* one of the commandments that surfaced was this: take credit for your accomplishments. I had forgotten that I had any, but in fact, I had quite a list of them! Here I was, full sighted, yet totally blind to my own value, my own worth. Too many times we push aside or forget our own accomplishments. Diminishing and sometimes ... transitioning them to invisibility—out of sight, out of mind.

My friends and family helped me get back on the road of taking credit for what I had done. It was their support that held me up during my time of need. And through it I was able to realize that the world hadn't come to an end. This was the beginning—a starting over, so to speak—of my next phase of growth.

What developed out of this was a lot of dialogue in prayer. In one sense, prayer didn't change anything. It didn't make the world more just. It didn't cause the grant agent to see the wrongdoing and come crawling to me begging for forgiveness. It didn't even change the financial notes that were due ... and now very overdue. What did change was *me*.

Prayer was the vehicle that took me down a new road, a road of peace. To create quiet time for just me and my thoughts. This was a road of trusting that in a messed-up world, there is Someone out there who cares about me. Someone hears me and understands me more than anyone else. And Someone can comfort me and best of all— surprise me!

Poet Ralph Waldo Emerson wrote, "When it is dark enough, men see the stars." My eyes weren't open in the right direction, yet in my blackest night, there were stars out there waiting for me. I just had to look in their direction so I could see. And there are stars out there waiting for you as well.

Heroes Speak

Winston Churchill was called on to give an address at Harrow School in October of 1941. The press set up their cameras. They were ready with huge rolls of film to record every word of wisdom spoken by this great leader. Reporters had come with pencils in hand and notebooks ready to capture the lengthy words that were sure to follow. Anticipation mounted as Churchill stepped to the podium. But rather than giving an extensive treatise, Churchill spoke only twenty-nine words. Contained in those words was his formula for victory:

Never give in, never give in, never, never, never, never— in nothing, great or small, large or petty—never give in except to convictions of honor and good sense.

And then he sat down. End of speech. His audience was stunned and then burst into thunderous applause.

In the face of advancing Nazi troops, Churchill stood by this formula. Defeat was not an option. Evil could not triumph. *He would not, could not, give up.* History records the victory won by his indomitable spirit, and the spirit of so many who bravely fought beside him.

Yesteryear's heroes are dead and gone. What about today's heroes who are alive … breathing? We are surrounded by them. You know several. Possibly, one is you.

As an author and professional speaker, I meet many unique people. People I would not have had the opportunity to meet unless I was speaking somewhere in a small town or a big city … maybe your city.

My heroes tend to be living people. I don't know them all personally, but I do know that there is someone I know who knows someone else. And they can make a connection if I really want it to happen. After all, having heroes, men and women whom you admire for their strength, their vision their spunk, their whatever, doesn't necessarily mean that you must be close friends with them.

Heroes like Sharon Komlos, who I met via the telephone and later featured in my book, *The Confidence Factor.*

Sharon drove home from work one afternoon and in a flash was blinded by a gunshot wound, assaulted, raped and slashed. And yet, she says that her faith is her mainstay. God has been with her and today, decades since her "incident," she says that her life is great. Sharon Komlos inspires me.

Heroes like W. Mitchell, who was severely burned in an accident that fused his fingers. Kids in schoolyards called him "monster." He went on to learn to pilot a plane, crashed and was paralyzed. Before the second accident, he claims that there were 10,000 things he could do, now there are 9,000. He can either dwell on the 1,000 he lost; or focus on the 9,000 he has left. The "W" in his name stands for *Wonderful*. W. Mitchell inspires me.

Heroes like Nicole Schapiro, who was raised in a silent convent for eight years during World War II before her mother was able to track her down and reclaim her; who was a revolutionary in the Hungarian Revolution; who negotiated herself out of a firing line at the age of 15; who convinced the about-to-be President Dwight Eisenhower to allow her and other Hungarians to immigrate to the United States versus the originally intended New Zealand;

who arrived in America with $10 and lived on the streets of New York for six months as a bag lady; who educated herself, eventually earning a master's degree and becoming the first woman vice-president with a major bank. Nicole Schapiro inspires me.

Heroes like Captain Gerald Coffee, who was a POW in Vietnam for seven years, surviving and being a key factor in the survival of so many of his fellow men who were imprisoned during his time there. I am in awe when he demonstrates his "Tap Code," the linkage that bonded the men from cell to cell. Their ability to expand their educations by tapping out foreign languages, sciences, literature and communicate—each man connected, yet separated by cells and walls. Every evening they would sign off with "God bless" to each other. Captain Gerald Coffee inspires me.

Today, Nicole Schapiro is a motivational and inspirational speaker and consultant who specializes in team building and negotiating. Clearly, she, as Captain Gerald Coffee has, has carried and translated intense wartime experiences, experiences that few of us today can closely relate to. Although Nicole was cared for and supported by Christians during the war, the nuns never knew if her family would ever claim her until her mother walked through the door after the war. Her story, the inspiration that she gives to audiences around the world, is awesome. As a close friend, every day I'm reminded of her presence with the painting she gave me. Sometimes I slip a rubber band on my wrist to remind myself to stretch as she does with her audiences.

When I mention Joan Rivers as a hero, many raise their eyebrows. But think about it. She was publicly fired with millions watching it on TV, and more millions reading about it in the press. This event was followed by the tragic death of her husband of many years. Her pain was immense, yet she stayed in the public eye, confronted her critics and took her lumps. Big ones. Her success grew after her public failure. Her strength to continue created hope for many. When I was a featured guest on her daily television show, her warmth and interest in my topic, my book, and me was evident. Joan Rivers and her tenacity inspire me.

Everyone has his own battlefields. Whether they are like those Captain Coffee confronted in Vietnam, the tragedy of a gas tank exploding as W. Mitchell experienced, the public humiliation that Joan Rivers faced, the loss of physical vision that Sharon Komlos once took for granted, the separation of family and death of her father that Nicole experienced—all are battlefields. These people had an inner drive, an inner strength of conviction, that spurred them on to greatness in the face of extreme obstacles.

Today, you may live in a battlefield—a different kind of battlefield. But nevertheless, it's still a war. The lines are drawn. Will you be defeated by the *noes* that will inevitably come along in life? Or will you, like Churchill, look the enemy square in the eye, with a glint of determination, and say along with him, "I'll *never* give in!"

The nobility of Churchill's cause was brought about because the evil forces of a wicked Nazi regime, led by a madman, had intruded its way into the fiber of history. Churchill might have preferred to be a lesser-known leader in peaceful times rather than to have had to conquer the venomous poison let loose by an insidious and narcissistic political power. His greatness is measured in part by the contrast seen around him. Even so, he never became stuck in his *"no."* He didn't get sidetracked by stopping at the *"whys"* of Nazism. He moved beyond the obstacles with great determination and strength. And he won.

George Bernard Shaw wrote, "You see things; and you ask, 'Why?' But I dream things that never were; and I say, 'Why not?'"

Why not? Dream big! See beyond the death—beyond the pain, beyond despair, beyond hopelessness—and dream of things that never were. Doing this won't answer all your whys. It most definitely can't change the past. But dreaming big, reaching beyond, can and will change the future if you don't get stuck in your *no.*

Within each one of us is the potential for greatness. Not necessarily prominence. Not necessarily greatness and success as defined by money or materialism or status. *But true greatness. Moral greatness. Life-changing greatness.* You may never be a politician. You may never be in the public eye. You may never stand before kings or princes or heads of state. You may never change the course of history. You may never pilot a plane, be in a POW camp, be blinded, be separated from your family or fired on TV.

But you can change the course of your life and the lives of those around you. You can change *your* world. You *can* make a difference ... in your home ... in your community. You can take the *noes* of your life and crush them under your feet and stand firmly planted on the *yeses* of tomorrow.

CHAPTER SEVEN

Is That All There Is?

*Once again, I was the unwilling victim
in a life filled with brick walls with the letters NO
hung firmly in the center.*

Never, never, never … in a million years … never did I think this would happen to me. I grew up watching such television series as *Father Knows Best*, *Leave it to Beaver*, and *Perry Mason*. In these make-believe worlds, families worked together to solve their problems. Husbands loved and cherished their wives and their perfect children. They lived in an arena where dreams come true, where fairy tales really happened. These shows always said truth outweighed dishonesty. In *Perry Mason*, the falsely accused always got his or her life back in order the last ten minutes of each episode. This I believed.

When I married Steve, I knew that all of it, all the dreams, all the hopes, all the fairy tales were true. But several years later, as I came tumbling down two flights of stairs—pushed down in a violent fit of rage by my husband—my dreams were shattered for the last time. All hope of happiness cracked with each thud of my body. Bloodied and bruised, beaten down emotionally and physically, I knew I had reached the end. That was the last time he would lay a hand on me.

Still smarting with the pain of my battered body, and the recent loss of Billy, I made my decision. This was it. I didn't care how ugly Steve thought my nose and face were. I didn't care how stupid he thought I was. I didn't care how low he had made me feel. Deep down inside I knew that no matter what kind of terrible person he had convinced me I was, I wasn't terrible or stupid or ugly enough to deserve this.

Somehow Billy's death had changed me. When I finally realized that I wasn't required to be victimized by anyone or anything—be it hospital staff or husband—I knew I was free to begin taking steps to change my circumstances. Rearrange my life. Not be afraid.

A job offer from a friend created the open door to my escape. He had wanted to help me get over my grief from Billy's death. It helped. Before the "layoff" that took my job, I had become fully licensed, but there weren't women stockbrokers at that time. Women became the right hands and silent partners of the big

Looking back, I can see now that there was a yes smack dab in the middle of all that mess.

wheels in firms. Being different from the typical secretary helped pave the way for my freedom. Plans began to formulate in my mind. Finally, after consulting a lawyer, I told Steve I wanted a divorce and I asked him to leave.

Steve left. But he also consulted a lawyer and within days, he had moved back. My plans began to backfire, threatening me with a twist: he would seek sole custody of our three children and destroy me.

One thing I hadn't anticipated was dishonesty. All the rules of fair play were thrown out the window as the battle began. Tragically, as happens all too often, the children were at the heart of the battle. All along I was certain that I would attain custody. After all, I was their mother, their primary caregiver. It would just be a matter of time. Yet, unbelievably, incredibly, despite their father's mean streaks, despite his vile temper, despite his drinking problems, despite his nonparticipation as a parent, he gained custody of our three children. Money won. How could this be happening … have happened? My belief in *Perry Mason* disappeared.

Enough Is Enough

It wasn't enough that Billy had died. It wasn't enough that I had been brutalized and beaten. It wasn't enough that I had been slandered in court. It wasn't enough that I had been victimized by lying and cheating. It wasn't enough that my family didn't support my decision to divorce. Now, as if all that weren't enough, I had to suffer the loss of my kids. It just wasn't fair! The resounding answer was no with a capital N. Once again, I was the unwilling victim in a life filled with brick walls with the letters NO hung firmly in the center.

Surprisingly, life didn't end, although I thought it would.

Throughout the trial I had been harassed at work—my boss and manager were even threatened. They knew it wasn't my fault, but I was eventually fired from my job as the top stockbroker assistant in a regional brokerage firm. I did research on stocks; worked closely with all his/our customers … even brainstormed with other brokers within the office with investment strategies. They didn't think I could concentrate on my work. My manager told me, "You need to stop what you are doing and work this out. Here is a two-week check."

I was dumped … and stunned with what they said and did. As I gathered my things from my desk, one of the brokers in the office approached me. "I'm angry at what is happening to you. You are smarter than most of us here." Yes, yes, I was.

The time was 1972.

Just before I lost my job, I was notified that my car insurance had been canceled. My husband had done it. Per California law at that time, he had the right to do this and just about anything else he wanted to do. And he did. He not only canceled my car insurance, he kept the refund on the premium. The agent told me that since I was going through a divorce, I was unstable. Unstable?! I was the most "stable" I had ever been in my life.

Steve also canceled the credit cards that I had obtained in my own name using my own credit from my own job. Gifts that had been given to both of us were transferred to his name. He did just about everything he could to wipe me out—including robbing me of the children and getting me fired. I was attacked on all fronts: mentally, physically, and financially. None of my friends could understand how this could have happened, not one. I certainly couldn't. Why would they?

Everything was going wrong. Then I got a phone call. One of the clients I had worked with called and said, "Several of us are not happy with what has happened to you. We would like to take you to lunch next week to just thank you for all the help you've given us over the past two years. Are you open next Friday?"

Was I … as in … where would I be? Arriving at the restaurant close to my "old office," five men awaited me. My caller owned an insurance agency; another was the owner of a large dental practice; the other three, all successful business owners. Two were "clients," the others were clients of other brokers in the firm. They stood as I approached the table, each hugging me. Whoa …

After our orders were taken, my caller started the conversation. At the same time, he reached inside his suit jacket and pulled out an envelope and laid it in front of him as he talked. First it was all small talk and then … "We are upset—angry—at what has happened to you. You have **In my hands was a door.** gone out of your way to assist us; find things; answer questions. Part of our success is because of you … the boys and I have talked, and we decided we want to help you. We think that you need a new start … that Southern California is too small for you."

Then he gave me the envelope.

Looking at it, and at them, I picked it up and opened it. Several items were enclosed. As I opened each one, they all started to chime in, explaining what they thought and why it was there. My head was spinning. Here's what my white envelope contained:

✓ A round-trip air ticket to San Francisco.

✓ A contact to stay with.

✓ A list of 10 interviews they had set up.

✓ A car service to get me to the interviews.

✓ $2,000 in cash.

✓ A note from a now-former coworker saying he
would take vacation days and help me move, as in
drive my stuff 400 miles north when I was ready.

Was this a "yes" coming my way ... totally unexpected
and out of the blue? Overwhelmed, all I could do was look
at each of them with tears in my eyes and just say, "Thank
you." In my hands was a door. Little did I know that that
90-minute gathering would set the stage for a new life;
a new beginning; a new me. If I was willing to take the
step. And to this day, I can still see them, and me, at that
luncheon table.

What did I have to lose? I needed a job. Steve and his father
worked hard at shutting me out of what I was skilled at. Upon
opening the envelope, I immediately started mentally
planning: Make the interview appointments that were
in San Francisco, Oakland, San Jose, and Palo Alto; call
the person who offered me a place to stay; book the car
service; and reserve my plane ticket. Initially, I didn't know
that I was being followed by not one, but two private
investigators. Overhearing a conversation between the
two when I was on the plane, I went on alert, eventually

waving to them from one of my appointments and wondering … why is all this happening?

After several interviews, I decided to accept a position as a stockbroker with E. F. Hutton in Palo Alto. San Francisco was old money and connections. That wasn't me. Oakland wasn't a fit for my lifestyle and San Jose reminded me too much of Los Angeles. Palo Alto became the spot—where the new kid on the block could fit in. At the time it was the hub of Silicon Valley. I knew zip about technology, but I understood growth. I would be the "experiment." Can a woman make it as a real stockbroker from scratch? I overheard comments from the male brokers—*guess how she will get clients?* And then smirks among them. What jerks.

I tried to pretend the pain wasn't there by anesthetizing it with twelve- to fourteen-hour days. How could this have happened? I'm a good person; a good mother; caring for others. I could hardly face the reality of it. Days blurred into weeks, weeks into months.

Did I make it? Get clients from scratch and build my clientele? Oh yes, the long, focused days paid off. After a profile was done on me in the local paper when I joined the $100,000-plus commission club within the firm, I sent a copy to my former manager with a note: "Did I ever thank you for firing me?" Never heard a peep back. The firm didn't know how to handle the "girl broker" … all the awards that were given to me were designed for men. I still have the huge gold belt buckle they gave me when I hit my first $100,000 year!

After the divorce and losing my kids (yes, I did), I learned that people lied, cheated, and stole. All with no evident remorse. I knew the heartache of not having my kids with me full time. Every weekend I could, I either

> **I had enough alone time to become my own person.**

flew them up to visit or flew down to see them. Grief overtook me once again. This went on for one and a half years, one and a half lonely years.

It was awful. Steve played all kinds of games, including sending the kids to me when they were sick. And he wouldn't be at his home when I took them back, causing me to miss my return flight home. In turn, when they were with me and it was time to take them to the airport for the flight back to Southern California, they would disappear, often causing them to miss a flight. As they told me later, they were planning on not going back.

The game was just about up. Steve had "won" the kids. All the "good" times were over. His ploy had been to get me back by withholding Shelley, Frank and Sheryl. When he realized I wasn't coming back, the game was over. He remarried two weeks after our divorce was final … his Plan Z.

Looking back, I can see now that there was a *yes* smack-dab in the middle of all that mess. The *yes* I got was that I had enough alone time to become my own person—a real person who was independent and self-sufficient. For the first time in my life, I was beginning to discover who I was meant to be. I was able to reach out, to stretch my abilities. I discovered new avenues of expression. And I realized that I had a purpose in life to fulfill. I had a path to follow, which was mine and mine alone, and with it, my kids.

Patience Wasn't in My DNA

It wouldn't happen overnight … and it wouldn't be easy. The process of becoming a whole person again took more than a year—perhaps the longest year and a half of my life. I had to wait for my *yes*. Not just for it to happen, but also to realize that there was even a *yes* to uncover in the midst of this horrible situation.

Part of one process included meeting John after vowing that the "dating scene" was not my cup of tea. It was downright scary. The rules had changed significantly from the early sixties. The year 1973 was a different game. I wanted nothing to do with a relationship and with men. One afternoon, I returned a borrowed book to one of my new friends and while there, I met John. He later invited me for dinner that he prepared. Was I impressed! Steve had never cooked dinner and did the dishes ... never! When John found out that I had started a girls' soccer team, he offered to team with me and be a coach. What the heck was this?

A year later, we married. The ceremony was in the chapel of his alma mater, Stanford University, in December with sixteen of our close friends surrounding us in the early evening and a chaplain who said, "I would be honored to marry you two." That was after multiple churches had rejected us because we had both been divorced. It was the perfect place. As a firm believer in small weddings, it just happened that my office party was the same night. I called the wife of my manager and let her in on our "secret"— that we wouldn't be at the party, but would she and her husband join us for a later dinner after the wedding ... and post-office party?

"Yes," she said and then asked, "how many are you having at the wedding?"

"Just sixteen. We will miss you being there, but we'll catch up at dinner … and, please, don't tell David!"

"Why don't you bring everyone here after the ceremony; have drinks and appetizers; and you can surprise the rest of the office at the same time."

Done … we now had a reception I wasn't planning on … and the wedding was set.

Remember, this is 1974. Our soccer team was excited; these were all teen girls. They decided that we should have a send-off party and they would plan it! Hotdogs and cupcakes … why not?

Oh my! Little did I know there was yet another long-awaited *yes* lurking behind the ugliness of the divorce. Ironically, it happened at Easter time—the time when death makes way for life. Out of the death of Billy and the destruction that my divorce created, something was getting ready to spring to life.

The kids were up for spring vacation when the phone rang. I didn't recognize the voice on the line. I was immediately wary, unsure of what was wrong. The voice was Steve's. He asked if I would do an old friend a favor. The hair was up on the back of my neck. "Could you keep the kids for another week? We are having problems." The "we" was the new wife of less than a year.

Would I? Not only did I assure him I would keep the kids another week, I added, "And Steve ... they are never coming back." And hung up.

Check and checkmate. A year later, I am back in court. My attorney advised me to not bring the kids; to leave them with a trusted friend. New hope with a new attorney. When I walked into the courtroom, my mouth dropped. It was the same judge. *Oh no ... this can't be ...* My attorney took my arm and pulled me in.

But this time it was so different. Within minutes, formal custody was reversed. That same judge kept muttering, "How did this happen?" Oh, I can tell you: money, power, lies ... that's how. We discovered that my initial attorney —one that would walk away with all I had in money at the time, had sold me under the bus. Double-dealing and setting me up for failure. I not only had lost my kids, but everything was stripped from me: no ownership in the house; nothing in personal items. In the crazy grand prize I won as a contestant on the TV show *Let's Make a Deal,* Steve got it all. What I got, which I couldn't see at the time, was an opportunity to build myself, and a life for my kids.

My vindication had come at last. But more importantly, my children were back for good and doing well in school. And years later when the kids were in their teens, their grandfather called me one summer afternoon. "I'm sorry … you were right to divorce Steve. I should never have done the things I helped him do to you."

When I told John, he was shocked after all that I had gone through over the years. And yes, I told the kids what just happened with all of them echoing, "You've got to be kidding … Grandpa called and said that to you?" I had never really sat down and told them all that had been done to me, including how the two of them attempted to portray me as a prostitute right after I filed for divorce—a distant word that wasn't in my vocabulary and an "occupation" I didn't even understand at the time.

A long and painful *no* had unfolded to reveal three very important *yeses* in my life. Having my children gone had "bought" me my first *yes*. It bought me the freedom and independence I had needed to pull my own life together. Another *yes* was having John come into my life—a kind, gentle and loving man who didn't dispense abuse with his hands or his mouth. And in due time, when the healing process had been given enough time, my children were back. Home. My long-awaited *yes*.

Looking back, the time I had alone allowed me to get established in my career, paving the way for being able to support my kids financially. And I joined the ranks of millions of divorced mothers. The judge awarded child support, but we never saw it. I had been given the tools to take care of them, and I was thankful that I could support them. That was a huge *yes*.

If I had been in control, if I had been God, and if things had been done my way, I wouldn't have made me wait for any of my *yeses*. Nor would I have experienced the pain of the past. My mind plays "what if" games at times, as most of us do. What if? If only. In some of my worst times, I have done my "what if" as in, what if I had never met Linda Briles, who brought me to her house one afternoon.

I would never have discovered my "Heart Mother" and I wouldn't have met Steve … and therefore not have had my kids.

And "Grandpa" left an important lesson for me. A "yes" that began with a negative. I'll never forget what he advised me when I was under his good graces, "People are like bricks … you build them up when you need to; and when you are done with them, you can knock them down." Something I watched him do to others, as well as becoming one of the bricks he targeted. It was one of his business practices. One that I knew was not a fit for me.

If a "what if" was thrown to you, you would probably decide that everyone should have a wonderful life. That there would be peace around the world, and no one would suffer through the disfigurement of a fire, or accident, or birth, nor experience the loss of a child, or a loved one, the terror of a rapist, or the destruction of nature. Nor would you make anyone wait to find a *yes* behind their *no*—if you were God.

But for some reason, waiting seems to be part of the *yes* process. You've heard the saying, "Good things come to those who wait." Good ideas take time to germinate. Babies take time to grow in the womb. Crops take time to mature before the harvest. Rarely does anything happen overnight.

By nature, we humans are impatient, and I'm one of them. In fact, when I was in grade school, I can remember teachers' comments on my report cards—*Judy is often impatient with her classmates.* Sigh, that was indeed me as a kid. And, today's environment seems to make us more so. The Plastic/Now Society wants it all. The internet bombards us with *get it done; do it now; buy this* … . Most want whatever "it" is yesterday; scratch tomorrow. When pain, hurt, tragedy, or loss are experienced, an instant Band-Aid is demanded—one that will clot and seal immediately. The Plastic/Now Society is used to the programming of modern television—a commercial break every seven minutes or so. Just enough time to take a breather, to get a refreshment, to escape from the dramas or tensions of life. But not too long.

Well, life is not a video or a show on the big screen. Life rarely gives a commercial break, and certainly they do not come every seven minutes. To be successful in the art of life, the art of patience must be practiced. Moses experienced generations of elapsed time between the genesis of a mission and the actual Exodus. And yet, he had to be prepared.

Never knowing that any breaks would come, he waited on the backside of a desert. Moses even tried to get out of it, but God said *no*—then made Moses wait. And wait. And wait. God's *no* to Moses, then His long-awaited *yes* served to bring about the emancipation of an entire nation. During his waiting period, Moses was learning and growing and preparing to become a leader of great strength and perseverance. It was no short process. Forty years elapsed. No one was in any great hurry.

Difficult as it may be to understand, God promises that when we look to Him in our circumstances, no matter how painful, how difficult, how unbearable or how impossible they might be, that somewhere, somehow, He will turn it to good. He will redeem it. Sounds impossible, but I have learned that nothing, absolutely nothing, is impossible.

To understand the *yes* behind the *no,* a step must be taken. The brewing turmoil of the past must be left behind—a move must be made into the future. The time must come when you begin to move on with assurance into the *yeses* of tomorrow.

How long do we have to wait for this to happen? As long as it takes.

CHAPTER EIGHT

The Agony
of Turmoil

*You know it has been something
that we all have been expecting.*

After Frank's accidental death, I felt that I had experienced seven years of agony in seven weeks. Words can't begin to express the grief and torment as we awaited news of finding his body. My anguish was heightened by a recurring nightmare—seeing it swooshing around … and around … and around. I assumed he would be found within a few days of the tragedy. I was wrong.

With my recurring nightmare, I called one of my friends, a psychologist. She suggested that I try and block it, to stop thinking that way—that it could be happening, or my mind could be a partner in creating the swooshing that I kept seeing. Geez, that was kind of creepy.

Still, the nightmare continued. My sister-in-law called to see how we were doing. She heard my anguish and suggested that the body might have gone out to sea. I then decided to try to speak to the medical examiner for our area, someone I thought would be experienced in this area. Connecting, he told me that with the time of night, the tides, the currents and the weather, it was highly probable and most likely that his body had gone out to sea.

Since Frank loved to fish and had been doing so since he was a little squirt, I decided that this was a fitting exit for him. Frank was laid to rest in my mind in the sea—a place he loved to go. My favorite photo is of two-year-old Frank holding up his first trout. My nightmares stopped.

Even so, inside my head I wasn't doing well; in fact I was doing horribly. Everyone thought things were fine with me, but I continued to deteriorate. Frank's friends needed closure, too. The day after his memorial service, several of them picked me up and drove John, Sheryl, Shelley and their Aunt Maureen up on top of a hill that was home to hundreds of redwoods. There, they had proudly mounted a street sign, *Frank's Lane,* "borrowed" from a Menlo Park street, our hometown at the time. I loved the thought, the concept that we had a place for Frank. Later, I called City Hall which assured me that the sign was now a gift—better in the redwoods than in a college dorm! Assuming it would only be a matter of days, I promised all the kids that we would scatter Frank's ashes up there.

Later that week, we asked all of Frank's friends to our house and invited them to take whatever items of his they wanted —bikes, skis, boots, shoes, tools, clothes—anything and everything. Frank was part of their lives, too. If there was anything they wanted, we wanted them to have something to add to their memories. Today, thirty-plus years later, it brings a smile to my face when one of the gang reminds me that he has some item Frank had loved.

Expect the Unexpected

I had underestimated. Several weeks later, I came home with two of my classmates who stayed with me when they were in town while we were in the same doctoral class. There was a message from my father to call. I returned the call and he proceeded to tell me that a reporter from a neighboring city had tracked him down. Frank's body had surfaced. I was stunned.

We had moved three months before his death. For some reason, the Coast Guard couldn't track any reported missing people, and the ID that Frank had on him included his driver's license and Social Security number, but the address was different from where we now lived. No one could find us, that is, until twelve hours after his body had been located by a duck hunter. The people who had bought our house couldn't remember where we had moved, so the reporter started tracking and found my father's phone number in Los Angeles, 450 miles away.

> **I sank deeper into depression, barely functional, spiraling downward.**

My father started off the call, "You know it has been something that we all have been expecting." I didn't know what he was going to say and anticipated with his tone that he was going to tell me that my mother had died. She had been sick for years. I had already mentally set myself up to support him. Instead, I was stunned with the words I heard: Frank's body has been found. It had surfaced and a reporter was trying to track me down. It felt that I had been thrown a curveball, from an area totally unexpected.

The visions I had been having had come true … that of Frank washing around in the marsh water. His buddies were relieved. Now they could get closure, by having his body finally resting up at *Frank's Lane.* For me, it was death all over again. I sank deeper into depression, barely functional, spiraling downward.

I called the reporter, who filled in the missing information, at least all that he knew. It felt like a three-ring circus. I also felt that no one seemed to know who was on first base. Records were missing. The state didn't show anything. The Coast Guard showed nothing. And the police had nothing.

He told me that he had tracked down a news story in our local paper. Working backward, he eventually found my father in Los Angeles. The other paper hadn't originally covered the story, although the reporter couldn't figure that out as it had been the lead news item over Labor Day on stations surrounding the Bay Area of Northern California.

After a series of bureaucratic hassles, I could claim Frank's body, and have it cremated. My daughter Shelley and I went down to pick up his ashes, a simple task, or so we thought. Instead, they were lost. It took the caretaker over an hour to find them. Meanwhile, as we sat in the office, the two security guards were like zombies, glued to the TV, watching a movie. An older couple was arguing between themselves and the mortician on duty about what to do with their bodies when they died.

Shelley and I just sat, taking in the entire scenario. It was crazy, zany, and bizarre. Shelley leaned over and quipped, "Frank would have loved this." It made me laugh out loud … He would have!

Finally, the missing ashes were found. They were delivered to me in a brown wrapped cardboard box. It rattled, a surprise. Little did I suspect that there would be pieces of bone, not pure ashes to ashes as I had thought it would be.

I took the ashes home and put the box away in an old redwood chest in Frank's room, knowing that they needed to be scattered so that he could finish his journey. For me to do that, I felt I had to wait for all his friends to come home, especially his best friend, Kit. That wouldn't be until Christmas time when everyone would be back for the holidays from schools and jobs.

The final gathering of his friends at Christmastime brought horrible storms. There were black, angry clouds … as black as I have ever seen them … deathly black.

Twenty-five of us trekked up the hillside. The clouds continued to gather. I had transferred Frank's ashes to a large casserole dish—his favorite for macaroni and cheese. Somehow it seemed appropriate that this dish be part of his transition to his final resting place. At the top of the hill, it dawned on me that I had left the dish with the ashes behind on the kitchen table. Down his best friend Kit and I came. We needed Frank … and all the time wondering: *Will the cloudburst hold off?* There was no doubt in my mind that Frank would have been amused. Somehow, forgetting the bowl and getting caught up with all the kids we hadn't seen for three months was typical for our household.

Could it be that the dark storm of my life was passing?

Climbing the hill, all of us shared our thoughts, our hopes, our dreams, our fears. We planted a redwood tree at *Frank's Lane,* a tree that did best in a "community" type of setting with other redwoods—just as human beings do. I read a poem Frank's grandmother had sent to share:

God's love is like a fortress
and we seek protection there.
When the waves of tribulation
seem to drown us in despair.

God's love is like a harbor
where our souls can find sweet rest
from the struggles and the tension
of life's fast and futile quest.

God's love is like a beacon
burning bright with faith and prayer.
And through the changing scenes of life,
we can find a haven there.

—Author unknown

After reading it, it was burned and dropped into the hole
where the new tree roots would be planted. We gathered
around. Kit held the bowl and I began to scatter the ashes
in a circle by their feet. At the same time, each of his
friends took a handful of Frank's ashes and scattered them
into the wind. It was a powerful closure and their final
goodbye to their friend.

Within minutes, as we descended the hill, the storm broke and it rained and rained and rained. Somehow it seemed appropriate. Could it be that the dark storm of my life was passing? The time for rain had arrived. And soon, after the rains, life and spring would come forth. New life out of the ashes of my cold months of Frank's death. I had been treading in turmoil long enough to begin the healing process—long enough to find the beginnings of closure. Now, at last, I could begin to move on with assurance and rebuild on the remaining foundation of my life.

If given a choice, none of us would choose suffering. None of us would choose the pain of death, of failure, of illness, of life's never-ending problems. Yet each person who has survived has grown significantly—has experienced a vision that he or she wouldn't have had without the suffering.

At the opening of this book, I revealed how raw I felt, and that Frank's death changed my life. He lives on in a profound way, for he not only touched my life, he has touched the lives of thousands of people that he never knew. Always, when I speak publicly, Frank is part of my presentation, the agonies and ecstasies of being a parent and the four gifts that he gave.

His gifts of:

1. *The renewal and embracing of the newness of life, of purpose.*

2. *The renewal of spirituality.*

3. *The celebration of my "little kid" spirit and keeping it in drive.*

4. *The resilience factor.*

Each time I share, people come up to me afterward, touched by Frank's four gifts to me, and enriched in their own lives.

CHAPTER NINE

Finding Faith

I was lucky …
I died and came back.

Years ago, I was critically ill, a victim of an infection which turned out to be caused by the Dalkon Shield IUD. Thousands of women shared my illness—some had just minor problems, some died. I was lucky … I died and came back.

My doctors did not know what was wrong. What was happening was my internal organs fusing together as the infection raged throughout my body. Parts of me ruptured internally before anyone really realized that I was in crisis. First the colon, with the bladder on the verge. I was dying. I could feel my body weakening and my mind slipping.

The doctor and his team didn't know what to make of the mess they found on the operating table. This was my third doctor, the other two pooh-poohing my claims of belly pain, of prolonged menstrual bleeding, and of bladder infections. The first two doctors had made me feel like I was stupid … a naive little girl. I'm sure they had pegged me as a hypochondriac.

Because no one gave me permission to be sick, I kept returning to work. A friend called to ask how I was feeling. Sharing my saga of the previous two doctors, she insisted that I see hers, a doctor who had completed a successful ovarian cancer surgery on her the year before.

I initially resisted. After all, two doctors had already told me nothing was wrong. They even told me that my problems stemmed from constipation. But my body and I knew differently. And when I revealed that the previous two doctors said that my complaints were minor and that the bladder infection I suspected was nonexistent, she insisted more emphatically that I go see her doctor. She proceeded to tell me that she didn't like the sound of my voice. There wasn't strength in it. She was now begging me to see her doctor. Her husband, a pathologist, had been referred to her new doctor by a colleague for his wife (my friend). And this doctor had a reputation of doing surgery only when it was necessary.

Okay, I knew something wasn't right. So, I followed my friend's advice and made an appointment. A few days later I cancelled it. The second doctor had called me and said that he thought I might have kidney stones—something that I had heard was indeed painful. As one of the world's greatest rationalizers, I jumped at the suggestion—kidney stones it must be. A test was scheduled for the following week.

Meanwhile, the third doctor's nurse called me back to inquire as to why I had canceled my appointment for later that morning. I told her about the kidney stones scenario. And she reminded me of the ongoing bleeding and the pain.

I shared with the nurse that the night before I had been wracked with pain, but this

Don't you feel these lumps in your stomach?

morning, I had felt better, at least in comparison to how I had been feeling. After these comments, the nurse insisted that I come in that very day, keeping my appointment after all. I was dumbfounded. Someone cared, actually cared!

For whatever reason, I did decide to honor the original appointment and asked my husband John to go along. Ninety minutes and thirty miles later, it was "meet-and-greet" time with doctor #3. As I sat opposite the doctor—before slipping into a lovely exam garment—I started to give him my medical history. As I spoke, I laid my head on his desk, then promptly collapsed and passed out. Now I was in trouble, real trouble, and he knew it.

I was lying on an examining table when I woke up. To this day, I only vaguely remember parts of what happened. I remember the doctor taking my hand and saying to me, "Don't you feel these lumps in your stomach?" Did I answer him? I was in such a weird space, not knowing what was going on.

I do remember his very serious and intense demeanor, and his explicit directions to his nurse. She helped me dress and walked me back to his office. I remember seeing John there when I entered and the doctor saying, "I normally do not like to meet someone for the first time and immediately say you need a hysterectomy right away. I want you to go straight to the hospital. You don't belong on your feet. We are calling to schedule surgery for tomorrow."

Surgery ... a hysterectomy?! I was only thirty years old. John and I were planning on having a child together this year. How could this be happening to me? To us? He said I had a huge fibroid tumor. It was the size of a six-month pregnancy. I knew my belly had been pooching out a little, but this? Now? Impossible!

Sylvia, the nurse, came back and said that because the next day was Saturday, the hospital couldn't schedule non-emergency surgery. "Could I go home," I asked, "and be with my kids over the weekend?" Still thinking we were dealing with a fibroid tumor, the doctor thought for a moment, then said, "Yes. as long as you stay in bed and check into the hospital Sunday morning."

Deal. I was relieved. Something *was* wrong with me; it wasn't a figment of my active imagination. I had permission to be sick ... finally. And I had some things to do before my away time from the office for a few weeks.

John took me back to my office and I told my manager I would be out of the office, but I would still work. Feigning that I was semi-okay, I cooked dinner that night. I explained to the kids that I would be gone for a few days and described the surgery I was to have. I told them I needed to rest over the weekend until John took me back to the hospital on Sunday.

Once I laid down that Friday night, I barely moved until Sunday. We lived at the top of a winding road in the hills. More than a hundred homes were set back in our little community with the annual potluck meeting scheduled that Saturday at our home. I told John to let it continue and I would stay in bed. I was so out of it that I had no idea that there were 100 people at my house—enjoying the gardens.

Things were getting worse and I knew something was terribly wrong, but I didn't know exactly what. The second doctor called that Saturday morning, angry at me for going to another physician and agreeing to hospitalization and surgery. To appease him, I promised to get another opinion, which I never did. My inner sense told me that I was finally in the right physician's hands. I felt that Everett Eaton, MD, was God's gift to the *no* I was surrounded by with other doctors.

By Sunday I was floating in and out, barely aware of my surroundings, and hardly able to walk. I said my goodbyes to the kids, hugging them and extracting promises of good behavior while I was gone. By the time I was admitted to the hospital, I felt I was going to explode. A wheelchair became my only means of transportation.

How could I be Mom?

The "routine" hysterectomy was anything but routine. The doctors were stunned when the the initial incision was made. Out gurgled green stuff. They had never seen anything like what they saw presented. I was septic. They were sure I had cancer of the bladder. My colon had ruptured, and my insides were like layered wet tissues, almost impossible to pull apart … to unstick. The hysterectomy that was scheduled didn't occur. There was no fibroid tumor. What there was, was a medical crisis. It took the growing team of doctors four hours just to separate my fused organs. The prognosis wasn't good. More like, "Let' s close her up and get out of here and just see if she makes it."

And I watched them. As I was transported to the operating room, suddenly I became the watcher. No longer was I on the operating table, I was floating above like the cartoons

I watched as a kid—I became Casper the Friendly Ghost. And now, I was an observer to almost panic going on below me. I saw nurses moving quickly to doors; more doctors rushing in; tubes being inserted into my body and just about any orifice that was available. I saw them opening my belly incision wider.

When I am asked to describe that experience today, decades later, it is as clear as if it happened an hour ago. One moment, I was lying on a table talking to the doctor, the next, I slipped from my physical body. Instantly, I moved from intense pain to a serene state. I was warm all over, all pain gone and surrounded by light. I preferred where I was as I observed the doctors in their attempt to revive me; to save me. It was a wonderful sensation!

And then, as quickly as I drifted out of my body, I was back, as if there was a reason to be here, not to have died.

What I didn't know was that I had been clinically dead.

Several weeks later, I went home … tubes protruding out of every part of me, and no feeling below my waist. I had to learn to walk and eat again; to go to the bathroom again. I had to take care of myself. My family was in shock. And

I was the primary breadwinner. How could I be so sick, so helpless? How were we going to eat? Pay the mortgage? How could I be Mom?

There were days when I felt I got nowhere. Then there were others when giant leaps occurred. When I woke up in the morning, it was a joy to look out my bedroom window and see the giant oaks that surrounded our house. It was a pleasure to open my eyes and feel the rays of light dance around me. It was as if nature was trying different combinations of her paintbrush as light flooded in and I waited for someone to come to me and say good morning. *Let's move your legs a bit. What would you like to eat? When would you like us to help you wash up? When … .*

Months later, my optimism returned. My lower body was starting to move a little; my bowels were going to work again; my bladder said "hello" one afternoon as my son helped wash my back. I was so excited to feel that sensation that I had to pee … my body was healing, really healing.

To this day, I know that there were tasks I had to complete. Only my immediate family and a few very close friends knew how ill and incapacitated I was. My manager at work didn't know. It was all kept quiet. John hadn't even called my brothers or even my Heart Mom. He was over-whelmed, barely functioning in the handling of the kids.

I had two phone calls I had to make. The first was to my Heart Mom—Joyce. To tell her how much I loved her. To tell her what had happened. And to do an ask: If something ever happened to me that I couldn't take care of the kids, would she step in and up to provide for them? I knew she loved her grandchildren, but to financially and emotionally provide and educate them as well. Stunned with my "catch-up" call, she immediately said, "Of course."

The second call was to my ex—the kids' father. He was told what I thought about him and what he had done to me over the years. There were so many things that I could never say out loud before. Now I was able to voice them … just this once. And I hung up.

I had plans … plans that would be rolled out for years to come that would be revealed layer by layer. I just knew it.

And the hysterectomy that I thought I was going to have? It eventually happened six years later when the pain from the extensive scar tissue took over. My doctor said he wanted to assemble the same team that had been brought for the first surgery; the one that had separated my organs and put me back together—just to be safe. They knew what they had dealt with. This time, I was quite optimistic, I had faith that all would turn out well. And it did.

Faith Is Noticeable and Substantial

One Sunday, I listened to a song sung by four of my friends, "In This Very Room"—so simple, so beautiful and yet so profound. Looking around the sanctuary, I was taken by all the things that had occurred to me in this very room. This was the community church I turned to when the need for a service after Frank's death occurred. In this very room, hundreds came—our friends, Frank's friends, his sisters' friends, relatives, even the curious. All were hurting, all were seeking reasons, and all were offering support for each other.

In this very room, we honored John's father who died just a few months after Frank did. It was hard for Shelley and Sheryl to return once again to focus on the dead. Yet, somehow, they did. We all did.

In this very room, daughter Sheryl married. Yes, "In This Very Room" is an important melody for me, for this room has carried great pain, fear, hope, joy, love, and faith. And faith brings it all together. All the pieces fall into place as in a master puzzle, a master plan.

Often, you see faith described by the metaphor of people walking into the unknown: stepping into a deep, dark fog and "believing," without seeing, that something will be there to hold them up. You may have participated in a "faith walk" or a "faith fall" where you were blindfolded and guided around by someone—not knowing where you were going. In a faith fall, you are encouraged to fall backward, and have faith that person behind you will catch you.

Faith tells me that in my darkest nights I will be able to find Him. And I will be able to grow, heal and turn to reach back to others to pull them to the light.

Faith Through Trials

Faith doesn't always mean you see the promise, the yes, right away.

Hindsight is always fantastic—it is amazing how right-on we can be when time has elapsed. The wisdom of experience comes when we look back. And the perspective of hindsight allows us to weigh the pros and cons, the good and the bad, the ugly and the beautiful—all things that at first glance, at first experience, may be cloaked. They may, in fact, be the opposite of what we initially felt or saw. Haven't we all been fooled at least once … or more?

There are those alive today who have stood patiently in trying circumstances—in faith. Centuries of history reveals the faith of men and women and of their religions and beliefs that carried them through extreme hardship and persecution. Stories of their courage and bravery as they endured physical torture, psychological pressures, and deprivation have been told and retold. Yet they stood. Unmoved. In Faith. Believing.

Faith Reaches Out

I'm a James Taylor fan. I've always found myself humming when I hear "Shower the People." Within the lyrics are words that are quite simple, yet poignant. He starts with a "shower the people" and instead of with water … it's "with love" and let them know how you feel about them—an excellent license for all.

He reminds us that we will feel better … I know I do when I hear it.

Faith is expressed through loving those around you. Comforting them, caring for them, giving of yourself to them, challenging them and just plain being there. Showering them with love.

Faith, hope, and love; all three are intimately linked. They are facets of the diamond of one's life. Faith gives you hope; hope delivers love; and love allows faith. No one likes problems dumped on them. But out of them, opportunities can arise. Imagine that. I remember hearing a leader of a successful and large organization say that ordeals they went through, to the point that he thought they would shut down, became a lesson … his leadership team, and employees learned patience over panic. The challenges his company went through and patience his team required developed strength, and growth.

The standard of faith that needs to be raised is not a standard of prosperity and wealth. It's not a standard of condemnation or rebuke. Rather, it is a standard of integrity and compassion. These are the standards of faith. For it is in loving and reaching out to others; and it is in finding and keeping faith, that we can change our world. This is not to suggest that faith is a compensation for loss or pain or tragedy. But it is an outgrowth, a tangible outgrowth.

God's Footprints, by Ken Brown, is a poem of a person, who looks back, reflecting over their life and discovers that there are two sets of footprints in the sand as life's journey unfolds. One set belongs to the man or woman, the other to God. In noting a particularly dark period, when everything was going wrong, the person notes that only one set of footprints appears. God is questioned as to why He left during this time of deepest need. God replies, "I never left—for that was the time I carried you through your most trying hour. Those are my footprints." This is life with God. This, too, is faith.

Faith Is Positive

When I speak to groups about the critical necessity to create positive energy, I usually ask a member of the audience to come on stage with me for a demonstration. Prior to introducing her to the audience, I tell my "partner" that at the time I direct her, I want her to think one of two thoughts. The first thought is total positivity: to let anything wonderful enter her mind. It can be getting a raise, good health, a birth, money, even a trip—whatever to her is positive and good news. When I ask her to think this first thought I want her to feel the thought throughout her body. When she has a "focus" on it, I then ask her to hold out her arm to her side, parallel with the floor. I then instruct her to resist my downward pressure on the extended arm. The result—enormous strength and the arm remains solid.

Now it's time for the second thought: total negativism. She is to let anything that makes her feel bad or depressed enter her mind: poor health, being fired, a divorce, awful pain, whatever thought is negative—not welcome in her life and her space. I then ask her to hold out the arm the same way and to resist when I attempt to push it down.

Negativity is like a virus to me: highly contagious.

This time there is quite a difference—no resistance. The negative thought has depleted her of much of her energy, of positivity. My temporary partner is always surprised, as is the audience, with the results. By evoking the dark side; by seeing just the negative; by not letting the good vibes in, we weaken ourselves.

CHAPTER TEN

Using My Voice

*The lies compounded—the State kept
deluding itself and trying to keep us
away from the site.*

I was at a local gym a few weeks after Frank died—a place I would drop into and let go. Let go by sweating and crying and no one would notice me. During a rest break, a woman approached me, tapped me on the shoulder and said, "You don't know me, but I know you. I'm sorry for what's happened, and I want you to know I won't let my kids go up there anymore."

My head snapped around. "What do you mean, 'up there anymore?'" I asked, searching her face.

"Didn't you know? All the kids go out to the bridge and climb it."

No, I did not know. OMG, no, no way is that happening. You mean kids have being going out there for a long time? Your kids? Other kids? After talking with her and exchanging hugs, I am shocked and angry. It can't be … yet it was. It was a "hangout" place!

I was appalled at what was in front of us.

I headed home and told John, "We need to go to the bridge and check out what's going on. I just learned that it's 'an attraction' for teens. That means the State has lied to us—there aren't fences to keep kids out. It's wide open!" I called a TV reporter I knew that very evening. She promised she would go out and look. I suggested that she get out to the bridge before sunrise … before any crews were starting to work (if they were) and take pictures. John and I would be there early as well. Later that morning, she called to confirm what we'd also observed: Neither gates nor fences existed.

As we headed out to the bridge, I was appalled at what was in front of us. Then, outraged. Other kids could be hurt. Purposely, I had avoided going out to the Dumbarton Bridge—I never wanted to see it again; say the name again;

or drive over the new one that had been erected the previous year. Never. Yet, here we were—two wounded parents at the scene of the accident. Approaching it, there was a gate; one that was flat on the ground. One that it turned out was routinely run over by the Caltrans trucks. All around were empty beer cans, and even diapers.

At that moment I knew I had to do something. I had a "voice" and a "face" that could be heard and seen. Reaching out to the media, I asked them to meet me at the bridge site with cameras. They did. Stories popped up in other papers, putting immense pressure on the state to finally do something about the deconstructed bridge—to fix it once and for all.

Stepping Forward

After we took pictures, the calls were made. The State Police confirmed that indeed it was a hangout. And the State Police had attempted to put pressure on Caltrans, the overseer of roads and repairs of California's vast transportation system, to close it off; to do something about it before someone got hurt. All they got was no response from the State. No action. Now it was too late ... at least for Frank.

Because of what happened, it was smack-me-in-the-face clear that I had the power to do something. In fact, I had probably the single most important voice to force action on the old Dumbarton Bridge. My obsession became dealing with this issue.

The call to the State was made. The spokesperson for Caltrans insisted that fences were always put up when no one was there to keep anyone from getting hurt. The lies mounted. There was absolutely no way that they could be put up at nighttime when the workers went home, much less during the day when workers were around.

The lies compounded—the State kept deluding itself and trying to keep us away from the site. Three weeks after Frank died, a gate finally went up that went across the access to the bridge with a "no trespassing" sign on it. Big deal—the gate was merely set in front of the roadway. On either side, a walker or biker had easy access to continue … as though the State decided that a "sidewalk" type access wouldn't be used. It didn't make sense. If a barrier is installed, then it should be an effective barrier. Period.

Unfortunately, when tragedy occurs, the "rubberneckers" of life will surface. People were curious about the site. Where did it happen? How did it happen? And the mentality was: Let's go *out* there to see why the kids went there! Let's climb, too! The State's response wasn't too effective!

At the same time, I was in a humongous business mess— a partner of many years had embezzled monies from a project that I was the personal guarantor for. By the time it was over, we lost our home and everything material that we had. Trying to save the project, I had placed it in bankruptcy.

The only way to get the State's attention was through its pocketbook.

The attorney for the project was a former judge who had called me and merely said, "I know this is hard for you, but if this was my child, this is who I would call."

The last thing I wanted was a lawsuit—to sue the State of California—me? But I wanted that bridge down so other kids wouldn't be climbing it—which is what Frank and his friends were doing and shouldn't have been.

Sigh. Forward I went. I called the law office and learned that there was a "process." The State just couldn't be sued— I had to get permission. "How does one get permission," I asked the attorney.

"By making a demand," he replied.

By then, I felt that the only way to get "the State's attention" was through its pocketbook. I demanded five million dollars for wrongful death. I knew that if I didn't go after the State, someone else could get hurt. And it had to be with something that would merit the State's attention, thus a large amount demanded. We knew that money couldn't replace Frank. We were certainly skeptical about recovering any monetary award. But that wasn't the issue. Action was.

Of course, the State rejected the demand. With the denial, a formal complaint could be filed. Which I did for the same five million dollars and wrongful death. Knowing that it was a long way off before there would be any action, I kept in contact with reporters.

Surprisingly, a call came approximately three months after I filed from a friend who had inside connections with the State. "They will never announce this, but I want you to know that the Legislature has just voted $4.7 million to take the bridge down. Your lawsuit did it. It will be announced tomorrow." End of call.

Not surprisingly, a few of the TV stations called for an interview after the allocation was announced. They wanted my reaction and heard that I would be dismissing the lawsuit. Who did they hear that from? I had made no announcement about a dismissal. Interesting how misinformation gets legs.

Whew … I called the attorney and told him about the call. He wanted to call the caller to verify. "Let's wait until tomorrow," was my response. My choice was just to wait and see what happened. In just three months, the State had announced plans to implode the old bridge and turn the main piling into some type of fishing platform. Businesswise, I was quite amazed at the turnaround effort that involved a bureaucracy.

When the implosion day approached, I had news groups circling for my thoughts and what I was feeling. Did I have a comment? Was I going to watch? Oh yes, I was! I stayed underground and on the Sunday morning of the planned implosion, we drove out to watch it happen. It was the major event that Sunday morning. Crowds gathered to watch the "happening."

A few friends along with John and I positioned ourselves directly across from it on a small section of the Bay. Sheryl and Shelley had formed groups with their friends to watch together—all of us very private with our thoughts.

It was truly a marvel. Once standing as a monument to engineering, its steel girders all powerful and impenetrable, yet the great bridge fell swiftly to its grave. A series of detonations exploded its base. It fell as I imagined Frank had fallen: suddenly. The entire tower sections simply disappeared into the Bay. Once again, I saw Frank in my mind's eye, slipping unconsciously into the depths. The experience was quite surreal, as if someone in a penthouse had pushed the elevator button for the lobby and dropped forty floors.

We heard a rumble, delayed a few seconds for time to carry the sound of the explosion. Then it was gone. The bridge was gone. Just like Frank. Here and real, one instant; enveloped in silence the next. My mission was accomplished.

With its demise, a thank-you escaped my lips.

The following Monday, I called the law office and said, "Get me out. The bridge is gone. Settle the case for whatever your fees are and close it."

It was over. I have no idea what the legal fees were. What I knew was that other venturous kids wouldn't be climbing in "this cool place" where you can look across the Bay to San Francisco any longer. Money was never the issue.

CHAPTER ELEVEN

The Touch of Spirituality

*I no longer needed Frank
to help me get through each day.*

Late one night, about a year after Frank died, I felt his
presence. Sitting up in bed, he was in my room, and
I sensed Sheryl peripherally. He asked me, "Why did you
wait so long to scatter my ashes."

Was I seeing ghosts … he seemed so real, yet his shape
was light. Responding, I said, "I had to wait until all the
kids came back; we could only do it once and Kit wasn't
home. He wouldn't be back from school in Oklahoma until
Christmastime. He told me he wanted to be here."

"Oh," was the response … and then, poof, he was gone.

For the following year, I would have conversations with Frank—just him and me. When I looked in the mirror, I could see him looking back at me. Consistently, I felt his presence by my right shoulder. It wasn't until a dozen months later after a midnight visit that I realized that I would no longer be sensing his presence. I felt lost. In fact, I was angry that he was deserting me.

Later I realized the *why*—I no longer needed Frank to help me get through each day. I was healing … and he had closed the door. I would make it.

It also meant that it was time for me to get closure as well. I was done with the lawsuit. My goal in filing it was to protect others. Mission accomplished. I was done with smiling, while sometimes seething inside with the inane remarks people would make to me surrounding his death. I never felt that Frank or Billy were in a better place when that was said—how would "others" know unless they were dead, too?

Bad times are not dumped on us to teach us a lesson.

Frank had helped me find my faith; he had helped me keep a spiritual vision. And now he could be put to rest … final rest.

Although faith is not necessarily positive thinking, faith is positive. Faith lends positive strength to our lives in our negative circumstances.

Have you ever walked into a room and felt what I call "bad vibes"—it just isn't a place you want to be? I have. Have you ever been around someone who is so negative in his or her chatter, that you see others sponging up what the person is saying, and maybe you? The term "mirroring" comes into play. When I had small groups in circles, I would ask someone beforehand to cross his or her legs. Within minutes, the circle mirrors the initiator's leg crossing. It happens and negativity is like a virus to me: highly contagious.

In the Introduction to this book, I shared how Frank's death brought me three gifts—one being that of renewed spirituality. This gift has been one of my most important gifts to be birthed out of his death.

If the wings of Frank's death could bring forth new life in me and in the lives of those who were deeply touched by his death, then there was a purpose that goes beyond the insanity of the tragic accident. It looks beyond the otherwise senselessness of his departure. To me, this is finding faith. It's mine to keep.

Are These Lessons?

A former friend wrote to me after Frank's death offering condolences. I called her thanking her for the note. She proceeded to say that I was being "taught a lesson." There was a "lesson" to be learned here. How could she say that? Those words slipped so glibly off her tongue—yet she had never walked in my shoes. She had never felt my anguish. Immediately, she went into my "jerk" column.

Senseless and dumb remarks would bubble up. Like:

> Frank's happier, he's better off now.
> *Who says … and how would you know?*

> At least you still have your daughters.
> *I was disgusted when this was said.*

> If you really believed in God, you wouldn't be crying
> … you should be happy for Frank.
> *What an unthinking and stupid remark to make.*

> Everything happens for a reason.
> *This remark sickened me.*

> This too will pass.
> *Right now, I'm in the present and I hurt.*

More appropriate is

> I'm sorry for your loss and the pain you are feeling.
> *Thank you for caring and calling me.*

> I loved to watch Frank coach the younger kids on
> the team. They will miss his attention and silliness.
> *Thank you for caring and reminding me how much he
> loved doing this.*

> I'm up early or late for you—call me.
> *Thank you for caring and being there for me.*

> One of my favorite things I remember about your
> son was …
> *Thank you for caring and sharing.*

> I don't know how you feel right now, but I'm here to
> help you in any way I can. I'll call tomorrow.
> *Thank you for caring. I look forward to it.*

The point is, bad times are not dumped on us to teach
us a lesson, but lessons do emerge as an aftermath. These
lessons become powerful tools in our daily living. God
wasn't "teaching me a lesson" by allowing Frank to fall to
his death. I learned to find a *yes* behind the *no*. I learned

how to find a spiritual vision—a purpose—to carry me through the trying months following his accident. And I learned that my voice could count for something that is important. I had a part to play. I just didn't know what it was yet. Whether my role was significant, filled with purpose and meaning, would be revealed.

When so much time is spent wondering why calamities happen—death, destruction, illness, broken homes, accidents, etc., we lose sight of the tremendous potential we have to effect change. No matter what end of the spectrum our *no* is on, whether it's a big *no* or a little one, as each *no* comes along, it seems like a catastrophe—it's *what is* versus *what I want,* or *what I can't have.* Accidents happen … they just happen. After things happen, though, we need to be open and receptive to the spiritual vision that will come in—if we let it. Not that God made it happen so you could see. But now that it has happened, look, watch, feel, listen for a message to come your way—to find a positive meaning in the event. Something you can learn, that you can grasp, that you can share.

In Frank's case, his death accentuated the fact that we're not indestructible. You can die at nineteen. You are not made of steel; you are not made of rubber, capable of rebounding.

You are not invincible. Our "forever" can be one week or nineteen years. You must live each day as if it's all you've got. This lesson hit home for me. I can look back on Frank's death and know I had no unfinished business with Frank. No regrets. We were in harmony with each other. Oh, there were plenty of times when I wanted to wring his neck— kid things that he would pull, mother-son disagreements, parent-child conflicts. It was Real Life 101.

When Frank left our home that summer night, so full of youthful enthusiasm and hope, there were no left-out sayings or feelings. For the past year, all of us had agonized over "career" direction for and with Frank. And then there was his service obligation, something that both John and I felt

Having a child die has got to be the worst thing a parent can go through.

would be an asset—for discipline and education. Frank had friends in the Army, and he didn't like what he heard. He really didn't want to go far away, halfway around the world. That ruled out the Marines and Navy. We thought that the Coast Guard might be an option. On the day that Frank died, information arrived in the mail from the U.S. Coast Guard. I never opened it, finally throwing it away.

Reaching Out and Through to Others

Book tours are things that were common for authors when I first started publishing. My book *The Confidence Factor* took me to many cities. In an interview with a magazine, a statement was posed that had a question behind it. It wasn't in my book, but he had tracked down a full bio of me and a list of my other books, discovering Frank's story. "Having a child die has got to be the worst thing a parent can go through. Having two children die … I can't even fathom it."

Quietly, I responded. "I used to think that as well … but it's not." He was stunned with my response. I clarified my comment by saying, "I think having your child abducted and never knowing the outcome would be the worst nightmare for any parent. Not being able to have closure and living in a never-ending sense of dread would have to be mentally paralyzing."

We continued our interview. Of course, I wanted him to write about the points in my new book. But I also encouraged him to do an article around tips to help those experiencing trauma or death of a loved one.

My tour took me to Cleveland, Ohio. A show that I had appeared on several times was *The Morning Exchange* and I looked forward to seeing the hosts once again.

That was, until news of a local tragedy hit me when I picked up the Cleveland paper on my way to the TV station. A familiar happening that spreads across America during May and June had rolled out the night before: the annual high school graduation. It was the perfect storm: graduation night, teens drinking and driving. There was an accident. Three of the "star" students died, including the president of the class and the star football player.

The city was waking up to this awful news. Family and friends were reeling, and I was scheduled to be bright and perky on the air in about 90 minutes.

Oh no … I'm supposed to be upbeat and inspirational … it's totally the wrong time and wrong fit for upbeat and perky. But I'm on a schedule—my publisher wants me on this show.

And then the portion of the Serenity Prayer I love dropped in:

*God grant me the SERENITY to accept the things
I cannot change,*

The COURAGE to change the things I can

and the WISDOM to know the difference.

Arriving at the station, I kept repeating it in my head. I
listened to the segments that preceded me. I was about to
take the spot on the couch. A mic was being hooked on
my jacket when I turned to a host off-camera and said, "I
know that I'm here to talk about my latest book, but I have
another one that would be more appropriate with what has
happened. It's called *When God Says NO* and opens upon
the death of my 19-year-old son from an accident that ten
other kids were involved in. Would it be okay if I lead with
this instead of the book we are supposed to talk about?"

His eyes teared up. All he could do was nod his head "yes"
and read the teleprompter as the camera light flashed on.
I'm introduced with the mention of the book I was slated
to talk about, and the book cover is flashed on screen.
After he welcomed me, I just took over saying what I said
above, "With the show's permission, I would like to divert
from my new book and talk from my heart. You see, I
too lost my high school son from an accident." I revealed

what had happened with Frank and how it affected family, friends and the community.

I shared the panic that his friends felt as they scrambled to find him; the zombielike actions that we observed and experienced as we worked with the kids; the news that took over our community on that fateful Labor Day weekend. The tragedy was even aired a thousand miles away on a radio show that a friend heard and the flood of calls that followed.

I shared how devastated I was when Frank died; how his younger sister who was with him needed huge support; how I was bombarded with the media; how his beloved dog lost all her hair; how I couldn't even remember to pay the utility bills or the mortgage; how even my marriage almost fell apart. I shared how I did all I could for myself and my family to keep from drowning and that we were a mess, barely breathing during that horrendous time.

The station was overwhelmed.

Oh, I knew the level of pain these parents were experiencing and the disbelief of friends and community members.

I could feel it in that very room—Yes, I spoke from my heart—I knew exactly what was circling around the families and city of Cleveland, Ohio on that horrendous morning. And I understood the shock that families and friends were experiencing and what would be cascading toward many of them as time progressed. I had been there and oh-so-done-that.

As I shared, my two hosts listened, asking few questions; the crew was frozen as they watched and hung on to what I said—what I didn't know was what was going on at the switchboard. Massive calls were pouring in. The station was overwhelmed. *Viewers wanted to hear more—they needed to hear more.* The producers were telling the hosts that they were bumping the next two segments and to segue to keep me there via their ear pieces. We went for three segments, two beyond what I had been scheduled for.

Leaving with thank-yous and hugs all around, the head producer approached me and asked if I would be willing to come back in a few weeks and do another show around the theme of Overcoming Adversity. They would arrange all the transportation and accommodations. Of course, I would and I did.

Upon my return, it was a huge welcome back, and yes, I was able to mention the book I was originally scheduled for: *The Confidence Factor* … one of the factors was dealing with adversity and failure. A full hour was dedicated to the topic and three other locals joined in—a psychologist, and two adults who had experienced sudden tragedy.

I happened to be in a place that wouldn't be a first choice for anyone … but I was there. Flexibility is critical, as is sensitivity to situations that we have no control over. My new book was the wrong fit, at least that week for the residents of Cleveland, Ohio. My heart, sense of caring and outreach were. Of the one thousand-plus appearances on radio and TV shows, those two shows are etched in my memory.

One of the gifts I received from Frank was the reminder to keep relationships current and in good shape—fate can come down and zap one at any time.

And you ask yourself, if your Frank were "to die tomorrow," how would you feel about your relationship—about everything?

Are you in balance? Have you left things unsaid that you will never be able to say again to the person who needs to hear it? Then look beyond. The person who died—what were his, or her, "undone" things?

We are all so busy taking care of unimportant things that seem important, but are not. It's a problem that most of us spend time on. Frank left some things "undone" with his father as well as his stepfather, the *unsaids* of yesterday. Today ended. Tomorrow didn't hold another day for him. There weren't any more opportunities left to finish his business. There won't be opportunities to finish your "leftovers" either.

No one is exempt from pain.

In discovering your spiritual vision, let your eyes be opened to the truly important things in life, those things that hold significance … real significance.

No one is exempt from pain. No one is exempt from problems. No one is exempt from being human. It's our common fate—a common part of humanity. Conversely, everyone in a position to help, to give of self, needs to step up and do it.

I know that the tragedies, the pain and the suffering I have experienced are not things I would choose. And I didn't. I do know, however, that I can help others. I have felt their hurts and their joys. What separates us from others is that willingness to give freely, unselfishly. It comes with vision —for and of ourself, of others and of getting in touch with your spirituality.

CHAPTER TWELVE

It Began with a Phone Call

I wondered out loud:
Why weren't they all here—
everyone involved?

I t was 1 PM on November 16, 1981. A banker I worked with in San Francisco was on the line. Short, to the point, his message was this: Clear your calendar and be here tomorrow at 9 AM with a complete, updated financial statement. And he hung up.

What? That was it … what was going on?

Clearing my calendar with my staff, I then asked my accountant to do an update of my financials while I updated her on my abrupt phone call with the bank. "This doesn't sound good," was all she said.

An ominous cloud was in the room when I arrived. I didn't know what was going on, but every vibe in my body said it wasn't good. And it wasn't. A catastrophe beyond anything that I could imagine would be rolled out.

Not only was the key banker there for a multimillion-dollar rehab project that I was one of four general partners in; so was a lawyer, an accountant, two of the largest investors who learned about "the meeting" and one of the other general partners, the one that I primarily communicated with and had become a good friend. For the project, I had raised almost three-quarters of a million dollars to buy the property and convert an abandoned building that was known as the French Laundry into a small boutique hotel. The monies would augment the construction loan from the bank.

Two years into the project, I am leaning forward, listening … and stunned. I discovered that the project was in deep trouble—that overruns had exhausted the construction loan … and that the bank had failed to notify me of a series of withdrawals that were based on my personal guarantee. Had I been lied to by my partners? Alarmed, I started asking questions. I was angry at the bank and at my partners ... and I wondered out loud: Why weren't they all here—everyone involved?

The everyone was going to end up being me: the last person standing.

The bank wanted money ... big money, as in $450,000 to cover the overages. "Just write a check and cover it," was what the accountant glibly said.

"I won't be writing a check for any amount until a complete audit is done of the bank's books for the project and of the project manager's books. No more monies will be advanced until the audits are completed. I want everything delivered to my offices within 24 hours."

I got hate and threatening mail and nasty phone calls.

And I left the offices of Bank of America, never to set foot in that building again.

After an extensive search through the company's books, we realized everything was in trouble—huge trouble. A large amount of money had disappeared, almost $500,000. At this point, the woman—my co-partner and friend—walked away and filed personal bankruptcy. The other investors, who asked me to take over, threw out the managing partners in a very public meeting that I had arranged with them all—a few brought their own attorneys. I felt obligated. I had referred many of the investors. If I could attain the know-how and learn how to run the hotel when it was completed, perhaps it could be saved.

Post-meeting, one of the investor's attorney approached me. "Your feet are hot … you better make good."

Yikes … there's quite a threat in those eight words. Years earlier, I had turned around a project when one of the investors and I had discovered a set of phony books were in play: a winery in the Napa Valley—one that all the investors mourned when we sold it with a profit. Surely, I could figure out how to do this one as well. I mean, I didn't have to deal with grapes, Mother Nature, bottling wine and selling it … right?

I got lots of support and encouragement, but I also got hate and threatening mail and nasty phone calls. I knew some who sent or made them; some came in anonymously. One I needed to share with my kids—all in their teens. Calling them together for a "must-attend" dinner, I read it.

The setting was a favorite—outdoors around the pool and a BBQ. The kids knew something was up, but since I didn't dump it out upfront, it was chow time. Then, I opened the details of what was evolving … and I read "the anonymous" letter I got. They were as stunned as I was with the accusations and threats that were in it. And they got the seriousness of the situation. They were told:

There's a high probability that we will lose everything. Our home; our investments; our savings; our cars; my business could go under—everything. Starting tomorrow, there will no more vacations; no more charging on my credit cards; no more allowances. Our lives will change significantly—but we will always make sure you have a roof over your heads, that you will be clothed and have food. Don't push me as this rolls out—I don't know what is going to happen … and I don't want any crap from any of you.

Silence followed … then questions—lots of them. Each one was answered as best I could at that juncture. My kids became my front-wave supporters. They waited up nights for me when I had late meetings. They helped more, a lot more. I had always been upfront with what my income was and what our household expenses were. As teens, each summer one of them would be my "household intern," meaning the designated son or daughter wrote checks for payments for everything. My intern went grocery shopping with me. Each child knew what monies were needed to run our household as we lived … and each one "got" that if moneys weren't coming in, checks couldn't be written. Expenses had to drop and fast.

The way we had lived needed changing immediately. Coupons for food were clipped and used. And I confess, we consumed months of just Top Ramen noodles—they were filling. Clothing came from the Goodwill store. I'd held off as long as I could before selling the house in a very depressed market. We became renters—first in one house, then in an even smaller place. It was tough.

"Absolutely. She is dangerous."

Anger couldn't describe how I felt. And betrayal—reams of betrayal. God obviously had not put me on the earth to run a hotel. So, I went back to school for a doctorate in business administration. My 18 classmates became my "unofficial" board of directors. They were a godsend.

The two largest investors and I descended upon the Berkeley District Attorney's offices with reams of data and financials. John always went with me to all meetings—he became my "official" notetaker so I could stay focused in all my conversations and dealings. The DA agreed—there was theft. We asked him if he would prosecute the removed partners who had taken the money. We were surprised with his response. "No," he said. "We don't prosecute white-collar crime."

"What crime do you go after?" I asked.

"Dangerous people," he said.

We all looked at each other. Thinking carefully, I then said, "If a black woman went into a 7-11 store and had a banana in her pocket and then asked for money, would she be prosecuted?"

His response sealed where this was going to go. "Absolutely. She is dangerous."

Stunned with his response, we left that meeting knowing that if anything was going to be salvaged, I was going to have to be the lead.

It was an exhausting two years, mentally and physically. We managed to save our hotel investment for the time being. But in the process of saving it, I filed for bankruptcy protection for the hotel. In addition, I dealt with scads of creditors, filed a lawsuit against the bank, slowed down my business to a snail's pace, and juggled health problems from all the stress. I'm sure the stress I was under was how my bout with cancer percolated.

The bank quickly became my unfavorite. We discovered mega-thousands of dollars were disbursed without any backup or my sign-off. I began to wonder, *who was sleeping with whom?* It offered $200,000 within two months of my personally suing them. Even though the monies were mine, they went to the project. If I had it to do over, I would have kept the money, and most likely saved our home. What the money in the project did was bring in a new player. One of the creditors created a "creditors' committee" and brought in another attorney. Whenever I think of this man, the first adjective that enters my mind is "slime."

He filed requests with the court at least monthly. That meant I had to be there plus the project's attorney. The fees mounted. It wasn't until I got to the end, two years later, where I had created a plan to bring it out of bankruptcy for the court's approval that the slimy creditors' committee attorney had to also approve. Within it, every creditor would get 100 percent of monies owed.

When presented to the court, the judge kept saying, "You did well—we rarely see creditors made whole … ."

The court, the attorneys, and the creditors considered it a successful bankruptcy. To me it was a colossal failure. I was broke. The only assets I had left were a few pieces of art. Basically, I had to start over. How did I get in such a mess? How was I so duped by a business partner who was a friend ... and a woman? Little did I know the next phase of my career was about to open.

The fire sale of all my assets became the icing on the cake. I wanted out of working with clients and their money and eventually transferred my clients to another firm and stopped doing what I had done for 20 years. I had been teaching workshops on women and money for years. I was in the middle of the finishing touches on my doctorate and the dissertation was on women and ethics in business. Out of the study birthed a new book: *Woman to Woman: From Sabotage to Support.*

That book, and my research that led to my doctorate in business administration, identified me as the pioneer in female-dominated workplaces and their toxic behavior. That book also seeded a career that spanned another 30 years. It led to over 1,000 media interviews; countless speaking presentations; speaking in all 50 states and more than a dozen countries. Where I thought my financial ruin would utterly destroy me ... it eventually led to a million-plus miles of travel around the world.

Ironically, it was a book that author Gloria Steinem attempted to persuade me NOT to publish. Over dinner at a conference we were speaking at, she said, "If you publish this, it will give them more to use against us."

Them meant men. My response to her was, "Isn't this one of the main issues why *Ms.* almost went under. Women were undermining women in your offices?" She agreed ... but still felt I shouldn't publish. I did—my attitude was, and is, if a problem isn't addressed and is swept under the rug, nothing can get resolved.

CHAPTER THIRTEEN

The One and Only

When the scars of life surface, some anticipated,
most not, it's important to keep in mind
that you have a lot of company.

There was no doubt, I had scars. And, so do you. We all have them. They are the reminders that we live in a human world of imperfection—a world where so many others are hurting and needing the kind of comfort that only you in your uniqueness can give.

Surely there are many people who can talk about God's *noes*. But only I can share with you the healing process that I went through after Frank's death. And Frank's death wasn't my only *no*. I have shared some of the others with you. I have a unique perspective, because my life is different and unique from anyone else's. As is yours. This is true when I speak as well. There are many excellent speakers and writers, but what I have to say is mine and mine alone. What I say and how I say it, may reach someone who couldn't be reached by any other person.

Celebrate your uniqueness. Bless your scars, even your weaknesses. And whatever your scars, find a point of thankfulness. Out of the turmoil and despair of feeling less than adequate, you can create a place of beauty—a solemn place of quietude—where you can retreat for comfort and strength.

When the scars of life surface, some anticipated, most not, it's important to keep in mind that you have a lot of company. Millions of others have and are experiencing your type of pain or disappointment. I know that this doesn't seem possible when you feel so down, and sometimes as if life is just not worth living.

Many "step" programs have been created to move individuals and groups along with life's situations—whether it's alcohol or drug abuse, excess weight, lost children, death of loved ones, work terminations, divorce. The list expands and extends in all directions. Most have cross-over value, so include common steps to get your life back on track, to begin building a foundation of living once again.

Of the many books that I have written, I find myself writing and speaking around a series of points to live by, to heal by, and to thrive by. This book is no exception. Often, I present these points in a decalogue format—"The Ten Commandments of ..." It's easier to remember and my audiences, whether they are readers or listeners, respond to their simplicity. With that in mind, I pass on my personal commandments for overcoming adversity to you:

The Ten Commandments for Overcoming Adversity

Be True to Yourself

In my book, *The Confidence Factor,* "Be True to Yourself" became the first commandment in building confidence. It holds true in just about any situation. When you stray from the "little voice" from within, it is amazing how out of sync you can and will get. Being true to yourself allows you to open up, be honest, defer suggestions, recommendations, even relationships that "don't fit" with who you are and what you are about.

When you are surrounded by pain and disappointment, it is so easy, in fact, often the norm, to be pulled in multiple directions. Advice may come from every corner, usually spoken in a louder voice than the one you carry internally.

You may even feel that you don't know who you are, that your life and everything surrounding it are off balance.

> I laughed along with the standing room only gathering.

Slow down. Take time to be with yourself. Work on your self-talk, your self-worth, meditate and pray. Give your inner voice the opportunity, and permission, to guide and nurture you. It's there.

Have a Sense of Humor

When the clouds are the darkest, even considering laughing at anything may seem totally inappropriate. But is it? My sense of humor has helped me in the bleakest of times. Laughter is one of the best medicines available, one that is totally free! So much has been written on the need for laughter in our lives, especially in times of illness and pain. When Frank died, it was often the little ones who came with their parents who put sparkle back in the air. Their laughter, playfulness, ability to burst out with song became a ray of sunshine in our hurricane of pain. Childlike joy is good for all of us and plays a critical part in the beginning steps of our healing.

When Frank's eulogy was given by his favorite teacher and counselor, Karen Friedman, everyone in the church laughed, and cried. We were reminded of some of the crazy things he had done and how he had brought laughter and joy to so many. When she revealed how he and one of his pals showed up at school one morning driving a semi-truck, my eyes widened and mouth fell open, wondering, *What— where in the world did he 'borrow' a semi-truck?* Karen went on to reveal his love of silly names for friends and his sisters and other antics that this mother was hearing for the first time. And I laughed along with the standing-room-only gathering. Sheryl and I both looked at each other and said at the same time, "There is something wrong, we shouldn't be feeling good at a time like this!"

The humor that was interjected in September of 1983 can still be remembered today by many who attended the service. It was a key ingredient in lifting the dark cloud surrounding all of us.

It was a tremendous source of good medicine for me. And it's a surprise ingredient for many at the most unexpected times. The Reverend Dr. John Snyder reminded his congregation that funeral parlors were not the places one went for decorating tips. He also had the "opportunity" to preside over one of the most memorable funerals; that of a man who had weighed many, many hundreds of pounds.

A tractor had to be used to move the specially constructed coffin to the gravesite. So far, so good. That was, until a crucial balance problem surfaced. And then the unspeakable happened. When the family arrived, the coffin started to slip. In the best Laurel and Hardy fashion, it slid—not into the grave, but down the hill. At first, everyone was aghast and then a few smiles surfaced, followed by snickers and finally by outright belly laughs. You can bet that no one will ever forget that service!

Take Care of Yourself

This is tough—especially when you feel so rotten. The last thing you may want to do is think about eating, sleeping, exercising, even stretching your mind. When times are rough, it's necessary to stop, take a deep breath and tell yourself that you value *you.* And that you are needed, wanted and cared for. When you hurt, it's normal to feel the opposite.

One of the surest ways to take care of yourself is to surround yourself and your family with *positive reinforcement.* People who are negative, whether they are family, friends, or outsiders, are not needed. Negative energy begets more negative energy. It permeates the air, your entire environment, even your very being. Look closely. Do those around you create positive or negative energy? If you aren't sure, the answer is probably the latter. Not a good sign.

If you feel that you are a failure, nine times out of ten, the odds are that you will create a self-fulfilling prophecy. But, if you think you are a winner, when you do fail, you are able to pick up the broken pieces, learn from them—and keep right on moving.

Negativeness will drain whatever positive thoughts and energy you have going for you. Moving on means moving on, not being held back. The energy suckers of life destroy almost about everything in their path. You need energy boosters, particularly now when you are more vulnerable, not people and more experiences that will be a drain on you.

Expand Your Relationship with Others

Indeed, no man or woman is an island. We need each other. And most importantly, all of us need to value the ones closest to us instead of taking them for granted—sadly the norm for many.

When adversity surfaces, it is quite common to withdraw, to become a quasi-hermit, to put on a mask—sometimes to put up a front that "all is well." It's not, so why pretend it is? Now more than ever is the time to reach out—ask for help, for support, for love, for caring, for understanding, yes, even for prayers.

This does not mean that you become a walking doomsayer, releasing negatives from every pore of your body. If you did, you would become the energy drainer of everyone with whom you come in contact. A "persona-non-grata," someone from whom others will want to turn away.

Rather, it means that you are open with your pains and hurt with those who know you as a person, who also know your accolades and bravos of life; those who can help bring a balance to where you are in the present.

Expanding your relationships with others during times when pains and disappointments surround you gives those who care for you the opportunity to provide what you need the most—a support system from people who love, care, support and are nonjudgmental, your true friends.

Give and Receive Love

There's an old and very familiar saying, "Love isn't love until you give it away." Remember how it felt when you received an unexpected note, call or a gift from someone? Sometimes it is a close friend … just an acquaintance … even someone you may not know! It can make your day!

Each year we made quite a big deal of it!

With the writing and speaking that I do, letters come my way. These letters tell me that I have made a difference in someone's life by sharing one of my hurts, my pains, my joys, my fears, my successes, even my failures. Someone has connected with some part of me. I save all these letters in my "nice letter" file. They are constant reminders of what life is about—giving and receiving love.

Each year, Frank gave me a special gift. He would do a *super-duper,* as he called it, cleaning of his room—usually an area of our home that could be classified as a major disaster. And he always did it on the same day: Mother's Day. Yearly we made quite a big deal of it! When my memories of missing Frank circulate within me, it's not his birthday nor the day he died that surfaces. It's the memory of this incredible amount of energy expended for me. Sometimes it was little boy pride that he would display. At other times he was quite boastful. This was his gift of love to me. The memories still make me laugh.

Stretch Your Mind

I believe that one of God's challenges to each of us is to change—to continue to stretch ourselves, to try to learn something new. It's like rejuvenating your brain cells, even giving them a new lease on life. Otherwise, you get stuck. Stuck in old ways, old habits, old thoughts. As the years pass, your stuckiness is like being surrounded with cement— it takes a gigantic jackhammer to break you loose. That gigantic jackhammer may come in the form of a cata- strophic event.

Learning something new creates fantastic freedoms. From opening doors and windows to areas, concepts and ideas that you may not have ventured into before. It allows you to transform some of your old wishes: "I wish I could play the piano; I wish I knew how to speak another language; I wish I knew how to paint; I wish I knew more about other cultures; I wish I knew how to communicate better with my kids; I wish ..., I wish ..., I wish ..." into real goals.

You can learn to play the piano, to speak another language, to paint, to learn about foreign lands, to communicate better—if you really want to. A wish is longing for something and never getting it. A goal is achieving what you set out to get, with a plan to get there. By stretching yourself and transforming wishes into goals, you will find yourself propelled forward. This is an exciting, and sometimes scary, possibility. As you move forward, you will be amazed at the changes and in your outlook, and your purpose in life.

Reach Out and Touch Someone

Everyone needs contact with another. And that includes you. It is well documented that without touch and holding, babies do not thrive. Adults are no different. We need to be told that we are cared for, both verbally and physically.

Hugs can do wonders. So does a phone call or a note that says, "I'm thinking about you," "I miss you," or "I love you."

It seems that as we grow older, we are more inhibited in expressing our feelings. Think of a small child. A child very quickly lets you know if whatever you are doing or proposing to do is liked, or disliked, wanted or desired.

When my grandson was two and a half years old, he had no qualms about letting me know what he thought or wanted, and neither did his siblings. He was also very bold in his request for a "kiss" if he felt he had a hurt on his body. He asked, and he got. What an enormous power I had when all I had to do was give him a hug and a kiss and his world was so much better, at least to him and to me. Somewhere along the line of growing up, we withdraw and hesitate to let others know what our needs are, be it a kiss and hug here, a kind word there. Or just someone to listen to us.

Reaching out is a two-way street: It's both giving and receiving. The more you learn to give of yourself—your time, your talents, your energy—the more you will receive from others. It's like love and marriage, pain and adversity, even peanut butter and jelly: If you give, you will get. They go together.

Come Out and Play

If there ever was a time to play, being in the middle of adversity is one of them. Yet, for some, it is almost sacrilegious to let play, humor and laughter cross one's mind, much less activate any of us. Remember that humor is one of the best medicines around. It has the remarkable ability to bring diverse groups together with laughter. Laughter and music have been medically proven to create changes in the body, changes that can combat illness and depression.

There was always a lot of play in our house as the kids grew up. It hasn't changed any, especially with frequent visits when our grandkids were little. Basically, when they showed up—play took precedence. Play could be drawing, reading a silly book, even cooking.

At five, granddaughter Bella wanted Sandra Lee

Twenty-three years separate the births of the two Franks.

cookbooks for Christmas … cookbooks? Yes, she loves the kitchen and creating. It's not work; it's play. And she got those books. Now in her teens, she is quite the baker and we love to see what she comes up with. And, when one of my clients heard about some of the things Bella did, she became a character in a children's book: *Bella the Baker Street Baker*!

Twenty-three years separate the births of the two Franks—
Frank the son and Frankie the grandson. Now in his thirties,
he prefers just plain Frank. There are four years from Frank's
death to his nephew's birth. And yet, I see a lot in common
with these two boys when I think of their parallel years:
both played with their toys quite similarly; both were
attracted to cars, any car. Both make up silly names for
things, are caring and giving, laugh frequently, love to
be read to and play hard. The Franks in my life have
continued to remind me to stop and smell the roses, to
laugh and play along the way.

Develop Your Relationship with God

Isn't it ironic that when people are in trouble; when health
takes a downward turn; when accidents happen; when life
just seems like the pits … that people open a window to
God? They do an ask … the "if you hear me … if you do
this … I'll …" surfaces?

Take some time each day, if you are not doing so already,
to be with yourself. And with God. My early AMs are
my quiet times. It helps settle me before plowing into the
day—dealing with the phone, the emails, the unexpected.
Quiet time. At times in the afternoon, I sometimes just

close my eyes and lean back in my chair. Assessing the day. I find it a superb way to ground myself. It certainly beats the negative news of the world and puts me in a fabulous mindset for whatever the day continues to unfold or for whatever it has already revealed.

Granted, there are some days that I would like to put in rewind and then eject, not allowing them to enter my real world. Unfortunately, I don't have the option, and neither do you. I have, though, learned to trust in my relationship with God, and to have faith that I will be able to handle what gets served on my plate.

Before every speech and moving to a platform, I visualize what I will be doing and ask for clarity and connection with my audiences … and to be there for whomever needs my words.

Years ago, I was speaking in Vancouver, Washington. It was Nurses' Week—a slammed time that had me speaking often at 7 AM until sometimes at night … for seven straight days. I was scheduled for back-to-back presentations from early morning to late afternoon. With me was John—who would take care of any book sales and just be there to help me. I recall one woman sitting quietly in the front row with a blank face—no energy came from her. It was impossible not to notice her, yet she didn't want anything to do with participation when I tried to pull her in.

She stayed the entire day. After I was finished, I was talking with some participants and noticed that she had folded a piece of paper and tucked it under the corner of my computer. Turning to her, she was already out the door; and she seemed to move with a little energy behind her.

After saying our last goodbyes, I gathered my computer and other items and tucked the paper in my pocket. As we walked out of the building, I decided to open it. After all, I was curious. I suddenly stopped and turned to John and read the note she had left:

> *Today was to be my last day of life. I had nothing else to do and saw that you were speaking at the hospital, so I decided to come and spend my last hours.*
>
> *I will be alive tomorrow. Thank you.*

My mouth dropped as I read it out loud, sharing the unsigned note. I called my host and asked if she had the names of everybody who attended. She didn't. I revealed what I had in my hands and asked her to be on alert …

one of her nurses needed support … and help. And my thoughts filled with her sitting in front of me to my right. I wanted to reach out to her; and we continued to walk, in silence to what I had just read out loud, I silently prayed for her continuing will to live.

Your words … my words … can make a difference. Sometimes you never know where they will land and what the effect will be. Thankfully, my words made a difference that day.

I was at a musical presentation years ago and had been mesmerized by the pianist. I remember leaning over and saying to my seat mate, "I wish God had given me the gift to play the piano … ." He picked up my hands and said, "He gave you a gift; in fact, two … you have the gift of words. With what you write, with what you say." Oh, wow.

Walk with Faith

All of us are aware of the horrendous damage and mayhem hurricanes, earthquakes, floods and tornadoes cause— death, families and friends splitting up, destruction of property costing billions of dollars. Countless problems. Pain and suffering abounds and multiplies. Yet, each city rebuilds, families and friends become bonded together, and the economy rises once again. Why? Because a foundation exists, a foundation that may be battered, but is there, nonetheless.

Each of us has that foundation: It may be covered with the crumbled debris of our past; it may be layered with the debris of the present; but there is some rock to begin to rebuild on. The foundation of faith is as great a rock as you will find to rebuild and restructure your life. It's not a foundation that you will visually see as you do a house's foundation. Faith, to me, is like the wind—I can't see it, but I can feel it. And I can see its effects. I know it's there. Faith becomes the working power in your prayers, part of your strength. With it, nothing is impossible. Without it, you remain in the dark. Lost.

Decades ago, the football teams from the Universities of Syracuse and Alabama were down to the final minutes with Syracuse leading by three points. The ball was in Alabama's possession and the team was within scoring distance. On the fourth down, the coach opted to go for the field goal versus an attempt for a touchdown—the difference between winning and tying the score.

The fans viewed it as taking the easy way out and sent some 2,000 neckties to the coach for what they perceived as "choking up" under the pressure. This man's name was mud on campus. Not missing a beat, the coach signed each and turned around and sold them for $100 each to the alumni, donating the much-needed $20,000 received to the football team! Overcoming adversity, whatever the adversity is, is achieved in a variety of shapes and forms.

You may be thinking that these commandments seem like common sense. You are right—they are. The problem is, common sense is not common. When you are in the depths of pain, adversity, and disappointment, it's difficult to let any sense through, much less the common variety!

If you build on the foundation of the commandments shared above, you'll be strong enough to weather any storm that comes your way.

CHAPTER FOURTEEN

I Had a Dream ...

If we did pull up stakes,
it would be a major transition
for all of us.

On November 30, 1989, I began a major journey. A journey that was envisioned in the early 80s after the embezzlement and Frank's death. The journey? Exiting my native California!

When I shared my dream of moving with others, their reaction was usually, "Why, you love the weather, the ocean, the casual, informal lifestyle? And besides, you were born here." But I did get "I don't blame you" and sometimes, "I wish I could go, too" comments.

I was born in Los Angeles, moved to Northern California during a horrendous divorce in my mid-twenties and lived in the Bay Area for eighteen years. Pulling up roots would have a few drawbacks. But I had wanted to move from California for almost ten years. Even before my 19-year-old son died; before I had lost everything we had built financially through an embezzlement generated from a business partner; before my health had taken a tumble; and before I chose to basically walk away from one of my businesses.

There was always a reason why I—we—couldn't … either business or personal. From being so busy that I couldn't see giving it all up quite yet … to the kids not wanting to leave their schools and friends … to my husband finally getting the chair of his department. You name it, there was always a reason why we didn't move. It seemed as soon as windows and opportunities would open, we would close them.

Throughout the '80s, I traveled quite a bit, speaking to groups all over the United States. It was easy to eliminate places I didn't want to live the rest of my life. Believe it or not, I narrowed it down to three— Seattle, Washington; Portland, Oregon; or Denver, Colorado; with a leaning toward Denver. Why? Contrary to complaints about Seattle's weather, I loved it. I'm a water person. In fact, all my books have been either started or finished around a body of water. The rain in the Pacific Northwest was not an issue for me. Portland is a city that I think works. John was born there; the beauty is stunning for areas just minutes away; and the coasts, a welcome getaway.

On the other hand, there were two key factors in Denver's favor. My work has me flying 100,000 to 200,000 miles a year. Departing from the middle of the country was a big plus versus the West Coast. Second, real estate prices had increased substantially in the Pacific Northwest. They had not in Denver. After losing our home due to the embezzlement, I didn't think we would ever be homeowners again … at least in California. Denver's depressed real estate market offered hope. A closer look was needed. If we did pull up stakes, it would be a major transition for all of us. Now I guess it was my job to persuade the family.

As Labor Day 1989 approached, a series of events had unfolded. John had been laid off from his chairman and teaching position; cutbacks were happening and just about everywhere. I had been writing and speaking exclusively for three years. With current bookings and my daughter Sheryl's growing marketing skills for our business, her recent divorce and the extraordinarily high cost of living in California, the time might be right to make the leap. Or, at least explore it more seriously.

Frequent flyer miles add up. I had several freebie plane tickets available. Convincing John and Sheryl that we could/should take a long weekend wasn't difficult. Grandson Frankie, just two-and-a-half, had already been on a few plane rides. He loved trips, especially with us.

We flew to Colorado, staying with my sister-in-law, Linda, from my first marriage. It took me one day to be convinced that I was moving here. The others were not so quick.

It didn't take long … I knew I wanted out.

Timing was another issue. John had just joined a startup company that would create, manufacture, and distribute products that would be used in science laboratories in high schools and colleges. He did not want to move. Yet. Sheryl was reluctant to leave her friends. Frankie just wanted to be with family. I knew that older daughter Shelley wouldn't consider moving at this point. She had a good job on the East Coast and had lived on her own for several years.

The campaign was on. It didn't take long ... I knew I wanted out. I felt like I was suffocating in sunny California. It was getting impossible to be creative. I felt like I was tied up and blocked in a maze of roads that led to nowhere. If I moved, would I miss my friends? Sure. But, as a frequent flyer, my phone friendships with my cronies would be expanded and strengthened. Many of my friends were on the road as much as I was. It became a minor issue.

Denver became my first choice. For someone who goes to work on a plane to whatever destination work is in, it was ideal as a central-type hub in the U.S. The cost of living was superior to California; it was an affordable housing market. A home that would cost $150,000 in Denver would cost $750,000 in California!

Utilities would be less in Colorado, even with freezing temps and lots of snow in the winter. Snow didn't appear to be a problem. Denver was well equipped for winter weather. Food prices were comparable. The only thing missing was the ocean. I could live with that—after all, Colorado does have plenty of lakes and I do find myself at hotels on waterways via my speaking engagements. I was lucky to make it to the ocean twice a year, even when it was just an hour's driving time when living in California.

Then there was the travel. John and I looked closely at my schedule the past year and speeches that were booked for the next. Over 80 percent of my speaking engagements were east of the Rocky Mountains. By relocating to Denver, I could shave 60 days a year off my travel! My body said yes … yes … yes!

Sheryl had just come through a divorce and she had full custody of her toddler, Frankie. Adding a new leaf to her life started to sound good. Kit, one of my son's closest friends, had aggressively encouraged her to go—get a new start, away from old habits and haunts … even some of the old "friends." To put the icing on the cake, I told her that if she would give it six months, I would pay all moving expenses. And if she didn't like it at the end of six months, I would move her back to California.

The major obstacle was John. He wasn't ready to leave. He wanted to try one more time to grow a business. I was on the road a great deal and we no longer had kids at home. John firmly believed that I needed out. That I was blocked, exhausted from the massive amount of air travel. He knew that I didn't love living in the Golden State anymore; that I had been open, even longing to move for the past decade.

We had to look closely at our relationship. Could we live in two different places and stay married? Since we had been in a commute-type of marriage the past two years—my flying all over the country to speak, returning between speeches to our home in the San Francisco Bay Area—we decided that we could continue in a commute-style setup. John would come to Denver at least once a month, a two-hour plane ride.

Before the next phase of the journey could commence, I had to find a place to live. For all of us. I felt that Denver was just about ready to emerge from the depression of the 80s that had been created when oil prices had slumped. Real estate values had nose-dived. If we played our cards right, maybe, just maybe, we might be able to buy a home and that included Sheryl as well. Almost unheard of for a recently-divorced 24-year-old now-single mom.

A few weeks after our Labor Day probe in Denver, Sheryl and I returned. I had found a place that would be perfect for both home and office. A full basement that had been finished **It was countdown time.** would work well for our office. We found it all in a 2,700 square-foot townhouse—three bedrooms, two baths, double garage. Because of the real estate slump, it had been vacant for almost a year. The owner was willing to enter a lease option to purchase it the following year. I secured it with the last pieces of art that I owned: two signed Ertés. This would give me the time for the gathering and saving of necessary funds. My dream to own a home that didn't have a monster mortgage was in my reach.

Because Sheryl worked with me, finding a place close to me would make sense. Not only that, being close and available for my grandson was a must. Within three minutes from our new home, she, too, found a townhouse—two bedrooms, two-and-a-half baths and a garage. All for under $50,000—unheard of in California. A shed costs more! For less than five percent down, she signed the necessary paperwork. The cost of her monthly mortgage, homeowner's dues and real estate taxes would be substantially less than what she paid in rent!

Not only were windows opening, doors were removed. It was countdown time. Nicole, my dear friend, honored me with a party one evening a few weeks before we left. Each guest brought a pair of candles. Lighting them, she or he kept one, I the other. I would carry their light with me to Denver.

Goodbyes and packing were completed. At dawn on November 30th, John sent us off with a huge moving van packed with two households and his small van with Sheryl, Frankie, and I heading to the Rockies. Both Sheryl and I were almost giddy as we left our home of 18 years. Frankie thought that the bed and play area in the van were perfect. The small six-inch portable TV that I had bought for $29 brought *Sesame Street* to our traveling home. Another friend, Yvonne, had packed a box with surprises for him—a goodie or gift to be opened every few hours. All was well in his world.

After crossing the California border into Nevada, the reality kicked in that we were heading to a new state we'd call home. Sheryl was leaving a bad relationship behind. A new life was beginning for herself and her child. Stopping overnight in Utah, we entered Colorado the next day. We were

Not only were windows opening, doors were removed.

all relieved, Frankie was great on the trip ... we sang more road songs from his Wee Song tapes than I care to remember. But we made it. Intact, not too tired, excited.

Speed Bumps Ahead

It would be wonderful to report that everything went perfectly, and we all lived happily ever after. As I tell my audiences, few things are perfect and rarely are things in the order we expect them. The move was absolutely the right thing to do. What a joy it was to watch Frankie grow into boyhood. Colorado was perfect for that little boy. As it was for Sheryl.

In 1991, my business went through some cutbacks; the recession caused many engagements to cancel, two book deals fell through; a publishing company went belly-up owing me over $80,000 in royalties; and a major company stiffed me for over $40,000. Would we make it? I wasn't sure. John's side wasn't doing well either. He wasn't getting paid and I began to put pressure on him to walk away and make the final move to be with us full-time.

In 1994, a court judgment was awarded for the moneys owed, plus back interest and court-related costs. Davida (that's me) had won, Goliath lost. But Goliath, like so many Goliaths in the past, didn't stop there. Egos, arrogance, who knows (stupidity is my first choice) became Goliath's guiding light. In the trial, I learned that dishonesty was a factor as well. Certainly, not fairness or doing "the right thing."

After the trial, several members of the jury stayed to talk to me. They were angry and wanted to give me more money. Why didn't they? The answer is quite simple. I didn't ask for it.

Why, you may wonder. I wasn't greedy, I just wanted what was owed. It never occurred to me that once I had to resort to legal representation, Goliath would immediately pony up and pay what was due. As my attorney said, "You performed per the contract, they must pay." Color me full-blown naïve.

Two years later, they did—the full amount owed plus interest was awarded. Never thinking that what I embarked upon was a multi-year situation at the time I started, it didn't dawn on me to add in the "wear and tear, loss of income because I was dealing with the situation" factor. If I had, the request for funds would have been a multiple of what was asked for.

Originally, I had agreed to do speaking and media for Goliath for a specific amount of money per engagement. In addition, we had agreed (at least I and my speaking agent had thought we had) to do several more dates. Never did I think that a reputable company would stiff me. I operate from a position of trust and faith. If someone says and puts it in writing that I will be paid if I perform "my job," I believe it. Most likely, you operate from the same position that I do. Most people will do what they have committed to do.

If I had had any hint that they might not follow our written contract, I would have added a few safeguards. If I had thought that once it was brought to their attention that moneys were owed, that they would have stonewalled me, I would have strategized differently.

The company I had contracted with had merged with another Goliath. My contacts were moved to other divisions. New players came on the scene. My contract was for three years and involved speaking, media, and PR appearances, travel, participating in a national study that would eventually be used in a book, and then the writing of a book for nationwide distribution. A book tour would be scheduled when the book was published and supported by the company.

I firmly believe that one must be flexible. During the first year of my contract, flexibility became a pivotal factor. The study was done, the book was underway, and I did PR throughout the U.S. The speaking side was altered. In my case, drastically altered. Initially, the company had wanted me to do PR, speak and write a book. When we first got together, that was the plan. Then, someone got the idea to do a mall tour. Instead of speaking at conferences and gatherings of working women, they thought it would be a good idea to develop a show—featuring exercise, style and yours truly speaking.

Where most people think of speaking as a stage or platform with an audience that is invited or registered, this one had a few twists. I suddenly found myself speaking to a transient array of adults, children and in some cases, pets! Their dress ranged from day dress and slacks to cut-offs, bare feet and skateboards. Popcorn, cotton candy, Slurpees®, and frozen yogurt were snacked on. Some would talk, get up, move around, arrive and leave all while I was talking!

I was not speaking at a regular "gig." One where I was the featured speaker, with a specific topic, an audience who wanted to be there and had planned to come and hear me. No, there was no disputing that this was an "irregular gig." Granted, I did speak about a topic that I had written about and it was announced. But there it stopped.

All speaking was done on a stage, kind of. In the center of most indoor malls, there is a large court area. Sometimes there is a separate stage; at other times, the floor is cleared, and a few chairs are set up. On a Friday night, and a couple of times on Saturday, I got to "perform" in this arena.

The announcement of my presentation was usually on a poster at the entrance of a mall, and sometimes in the weekly throw-away advertising paper. Many of my audiences were there because they stumbled across the center court in the mall and decided to stop for a few minutes and listen in.

What a joke. I hated what I was doing. It was a total misuse of my skills and talents. Could I speak to a crowd? You bet. Normally, my audiences ranged from 50 to 5,000. Evaluations were always excellent.

What happened here? It wasn't that I didn't care for my audience, nor that the audience disliked what they heard. The audience had a good time, but I didn't; at least on the inside, in my heart. This was the wrong fit.

I am quite certain that being a shopping mall speaker wasn't my purpose in life. I will admit that the experience (over 80 talks in the center court of countless malls) enhanced my speaking skills. But that wasn't what I had signed on for. I was thrilled when I gave my last mall appearance.

Then, I waited. The company had promised that I wouldn't be speaking in malls anymore, and that the women's working market would now be targeted. Future speeches would be done for professional conferences and meetings. Finally, I would be used in the right place. Then directions changed again. New definitions surfaced. Goliath proclaimed that speaking in malls wasn't speaking; instead, it was doing PR for the book. Therefore, all the work I had done during the year was "free."

Huh?

I couldn't believe the company's attitude. I had done the work, even more than I had ever agreed to in the beginning. I know I was owed $40,000, plus expenses. Being stunned was an understatement. One of the original corporate employees no longer worked for Goliath. When she heard that I hadn't been paid, she was outraged. She encouraged me to contact the president of the company directly. "Bill was elated with the success of the campaign that you did for us. Contact him ... I know he will want you paid." Reluctantly, I did.

It took me three days to write a two-page letter with just the facts. I offered a compromise. The company still had two to three thousand copies of the book I had written. I suggested that those books be given to me in lieu of the moneys owed. Over the next few years, I would sell them at my regular speaking engagements and eventually recoup the money owed. In the meanwhile, I would still be a vocal supporter of the company and its products. I ended my letter with, "Can we talk?"

In a word, "Nope." I received a fax that said three things. One, I must apologize. Two, I must withdraw my demands (there were none in my letter!). Three, if I did not do one and two, a threat was introduced: I would never work for a big company again.

Okay, that was the button pusher for me! Off I went to an attorney with that fax in hand. When he reviewed my files, correspondence and my contract, he said that it was really a simple matter—a breach of contract. A demand letter was sent to Goliath for the moneys owed. I told my attorney that if they offered $25,000, take it and close the matter. The demand letter was ignored.

One side of me wanted to walk away. As you read *When God Says NO*, you know I have had my share of potholes. The last thing I wanted to do was enter a lawsuit. I had gone through an embezzlement that sapped my time, my energy, my health, my bank account, my investments, my business, and many friend and business relationships— just about my everything. There were lawsuits, attorneys draining the last of any assets I had—I was broke and had to rebuild everything from scratch. One day, I longed to own the home I was leasing.

But, as one of my women friends said, "This is not okay. You worked. You honored the contract and the additional requests that they verbally added to it. They were able to measure the amount of publicity that your media appearances generated. They owe it to you. And you owe it to other women who have been run over by big bureaucracies when it comes to equitable pay."

A lawsuit was filed. I never thought it would end up in a court room, but it did. Not once, but twice. When Goliath lost in the jury trial, they appealed the ruling. Because I never thought it would end up in a trial, lawyers' fees were never requested or the amount of down time I experienced because of the situation factored in. That was a mistake. It took several years from the time I filed the lawsuit to the time I collected the money.

The total cost to Goliath was in excess of four times what they owed me. What a tremendous waste of everyone's time. And money. And here's what we learned: I had been paid—it was sent to the PR firm. They kept it … basically stole my money and had to cough it up. I often wonder, how many would pursue a scenario like this as I did? After all, I was prepared to walk away when it first became clear that I wouldn't be paid. I didn't want another hassle, a pothole in my life.

Eventually, the company John currently worked for was not able to pay the back salary owed him, even sticking some of the outstanding debt in his lap. "Get out of California now," was all I could say. "I expect to see you by the end of the week." We felt like we were surrounded by Noes. Everywhere.

It would have been easy to slip into a "woe is me and woe is us" cycle. To concentrate on the Noes, forgetting and blocking the Yeses that were out there. But only if we would be open to them. We were not. It was time to roll up our sleeves and dig in.

On the plus side, we were able to convince the owner of our home to wait another year for the purchase to occur. It took a full year to rebuild and get my speaking business growing again. After moving to Colorado, John needed some time to heal his wounds—and yes, his ego and physical well-being. The stress of living the way we had been, along with the business failing, was crushing.

And what of my other daughter, Shelley? She, too, was now living and working in Colorado, having secured a position with the same company.

Now we were all here. A family. A good thing.

CHAPTER FIFTEEN

Miracles Do Happen!

Pain is inevitable …
misery is not. This I believe.

My three years were almost up. I could hardly wait to end my term on the ruling board of my church, something that I wanted ending at the top of my "stop-doing-this" list. A lot had happened over the three years—major changes, major upheavals, major pain as well as a continued probe and expansion of my own spirituality.

At the last board session meeting just prior to Thanksgiving, we all went around the room sharing what we were thankful for. If I had received the letter from the foster child that John and I had taken in the year before prior to that meeting, I would have shared it. By the following Sunday, though, the letter was in my hands and I was able to share it with the entire congregation as I made my final presentation for our stewardship drive.

The girl who wrote the letter was thirteen going on thirty-three when she came into our lives. The year before, John and I, unsuspecting of the roles we were about to play, had stopped by our friend Cathy's home to pick up a video. Her granddaughter was visiting, a girl whom we had known since she was a little tyke. Now there were problems.

Almost by definition, teens have problems. Jessica appeared to have an extra dose. Her handling of them and herself, along with her interactions with her family and school, were not acceptable. She had become a one-person anti-everything—school, society, family. The previous Christmas, she had spent the holidays in Juvenile Hall. She had stolen material items, money, credit cards; she had been drinking and using pot. Her grandmother had taken her in, but unknown to John and me, was at the end of her rope.

After our usual greetings, I asked my friend if she had seen a certain movie. She hadn't. I suggested we all go and take Jessica with us. "Jessica's not going anywhere," snapped Cathy.

Something was wrong here. The storm unfolded. Jessica was drinking and couldn't be trusted for anything. Cathy had caught her sneaking back in after a "night" out. Jessica had made her own life miserable, and now she was making everyone else's life miserable as well. She had endangered her little brother.

You really blew it, didn't you?

Cathy had had it. She would not be lied to anymore. The pain of her daughter's death due to drugs was overwhelming. When she saw her granddaughter heading down the same path as Lori had, she couldn't bear it. She had wanted desperately to help Jessica through this period. And yet, here was Jessica, telling the same lies and stories as her daughter had.

For Cathy, it was déjà vu. The nightmare for my friend continued. She was throwing in the towel. She had done all she could do with the tools she had. She felt Jessica needed something, but she apparently wasn't that something.

Instead of just picking up the video, we stayed for dinner. Since our ten-minute stopover was going to last a few hours, I decided to go and take a quick glance at the video. Jessica followed me into the bedroom and crawled on the bed with me. My first words were, "You really blew it, didn't you?" Her response was, "The others made me do it."

Oh my, I heard those words spill out from so many kids, and I didn't believe her. For the next two hours, I talked with Jessica, confronting her gently, sometimes not so gently. If she was ever going to get her act together, taking responsibility was a key ingredient.

Before she went to bed that night, John joined me and listened in. He recited to her the poem about courage from Winnie the Pooh. It ends with: "Don't give up hope." She made promises. Jessica seemed encouraged.

Her family wasn't, though. They were at their wit's end with that girl. And I couldn't blame them. We knew what it was like. We knew what the sneaking in and out was all about. What the never-ending lies that created complicated webs were all about. We had gone through the drug routine with one of my kids. It was hell for us—some of those teen years. John and I took turns sleeping at night. We didn't know if we would have a house standing the next morning if we both slept at the same time.

Our ten-minute stopover that started at six PM went on to one AM. We talked with Cathy and Jessica. Mostly, we listened. This was one of my best friends and she was hurting big-time. I hated to see her so torn, so vulnerable. Cathy was going to call Jessica's probation officer the next day. If Jessica went to a foster home, it would be her problem, her choice. Cathy could do no more.

Both John and I hated to see what was unfolding in front of our us. We didn't want to see Jessica tumbled around by the system, and we were convinced that it would not be the solution to her problems. Late into that evening and early morning, we talked. Perhaps if we took her in for a few weeks, things would slow down. Everyone would cool off. Get better. It would certainly take the immediate pressure off Cathy, and then maybe Jessica could move back in with her.

That's not how the system worked. We couldn't take her for a couple of weeks—we had to either take her for five or six months or not at all. And we had to be approved as foster parents by the county. Finally, we felt there was no choice. We knew we had to do it. We entered the foster family system.

I called Cathy the next morning and asked her if she had an hour—that I would be over in fifteen minutes. Upon arriving, I drove her to a school that had done wonders for two of my kids—turnarounds for them both: Frank, who was dyslexic and struggling at school, and his younger sister, who had no fear. She would try anything—daredevil or experimental.

Both had graduated, were whole human beings, having done major about-faces. After meeting with the principal and a counselor, I asked Cathy if she would be willing to pay fall tuition for the private school if John and I agreed to be Jessica's foster parents. And, I had a therapist I wanted her to work with—would she cover the costs? Never hesitating, she said she would.

Having gone through it with our kids, we knew what we were in for. Rules had to be made … and kept. We were willing to let Jessica come if both she and her family agreed to our rules: she would have to go to the school of our choice; she would not be in contact with her parents or grandmother for thirty days; she would have to go to the therapist of our choice, a therapist who had helped John and me restore our marriage as well as someone who specialized in chemical abuse by teens; she would go to church with us; and she would have to go to work for me after school. Plus, my staff had to be behind her being there one hundred percent. If I was away on business, they in fact became surrogate foster mothers. Finally, her family would have to put new locks on our home, so it was both break-in and break-out proof.

Booze and drugs do a lot of talking—and we weren't about to listen.

The night before Jessica officially arrived on our doorstep, she attempted suicide. The day before she had learned that she would be living with us; she had also learned the day before that she was going to a new therapist, the therapist of our choice. Both were fine with her. What she hadn't been told by her parents and grandmother was that she would not be going to the same school. A new one, a school of my choice, was her only option.

Jessica was furious. Her reaction was to drink the booze she had stashed and to cut her wrists. She then called me after the deed was done. I, in turn, called the new therapist. How Cathy stayed uninvolved, almost oblivious to Jessica's trauma/drama unfolding in another part of her home, I'm not sure. But she did.

When Jessica called me and told me of her *deed*, I took off for Cathy's home, five minutes away. I was able to determine that her cuts were not physically life-threatening; had a medical doctor check her and proceeded to have her bandaged up. I called the therapist and had Jessica talk to him. The next morning, we both were in his office first thing. That was followed up with a visit to Planned Parenthood for a full physical.

Between the mental doctor, the medical doctor, and me, the caring doctor, we made it through that first day, the first week. Cutting her wrists was not effective enough to take her life. It was effective in saying she needed help—plenty of it.

Honeymoons don't last forever.

For the first few months, Jessica was in love with me. We restored some privileges as time passed. She started doing well in school.

And she started to make new friends. I must add that despite her improvements, things were not as smooth as

I thought they would be. Jessica's presence created havoc with my oldest daughter Shelley, who was sure we were suffering from "empty nest syndrome" and out of our minds for bringing this problem into our home, our lives. I was not prepared, nor did I ever anticipate, that I would be confronted with sibling rivalry at this stage of my life. After all, my daughters were twenty-four and twenty. But that's what it was.

Shelley wasn't happy that Jessica was firmly entrenched in our home. It's not that Jessica had taken over her old room or used any of her things, at least not directly. What Jessica had done was this: she possessed us. John and I couldn't do anything without making plans for Jessica; she went everywhere with us. Or, we stayed home and had friends over. Our friends supported us in supporting Jessica … and our attempt to help her.

Honeymoons don't last forever. Ours was no exception. For many parents of teens, there is often the "lull before the storm." Four months after Jessica arrived, we allowed her to stay overnight with one of her school friends. We had a phone number, names of parents. I even called the school to ask about the other girl and her family. John and

I looked forward to being with each other, a night off we both felt we had earned.

A few weeks later, Jessica asked again if she could stay over and go to a barbecue. After checking with parents and about the barbecue host, we found that the facts did not fit! We didn't get a one-plus-one equation. It was full of fractions. I called her grandmother and suggested that we have a physical checkup on her. I was suspicious of drugs.

One of our initial rules was that if there was any doubt on my part, Jessica would have to go to Alcoholics Anonymous and/or Narcotics Anonymous. Attendance at these meetings would be the consequence of what John and I deemed suspicious behavior; no real proof was needed. If we said she had to go, she had to go. Her therapist backed us up.

Miss Jessica tested positive and I knew that meeting time was in order. There were several locations and times to choose from. Most meetings were held at local churches in our immediate area. Originally, I hadn't planned to attend these meetings, but here I found myself weekly, sitting with Jessica in a smoke-filled room. My allergies crawled up the walls to escape the smell of the smoke. She fought going in the first place … and we reminded her of the rules, the rules that she okayed from the get-go. The rules that if they were broken; that she did them by *her* choice.

Approximately six months after Jessica arrived, she went home … always the primary goal for her family and for us. All of them had been in therapy; sometimes alone, sometimes together for the past six months. They had learned a lot about each other. There was still more to come. But they were talking to each other, a breakthrough. They were working together, and I made the call to my liaison with foster care, sharing that she was ready … and we were closing out. Literally, they begged us to take more troubled teens—they needed families who understood them and could work with them.

Raising kids is work; troubled kids more so. More work, increasing travel, and commitments weren't going to allow it. We were grateful to be there for a young girl who was desperate. John and I don't believe in throwing kids under the bus if we can help. But now, we—I—needed to refocus. My gift to my friend Cathy and to Jessica had been to be there in this time.

Thank you for saving my life.

At one point, Jessica's suicide attempt had me calling for help while I was nursing her wounds and trying to keep her alive, wondering if I was out of my mind. So that Thanksgiving, after her letter arrived, I knew that all the hassles and trials of trying to get Jessica to straighten out, of trying to make a difference in her life, had been worth it. "Thank you for saving my life," she wrote.

Jessica had been resurrected! The probation department was pleased with her progress. So were her parents and her therapist. That's what caring and sharing are all about. That's what being a human being is all about.

Another Teen Needs Help

Little did I know that "a déjà vu" would resurrect again decades later. When Jessica had arrived on our doorstep, I was in my 30s; when I took the next teen into our home, I was in my late 50s—quite a gap. This time it was my family … and my grandson. Frankie is 19 and now "Frank" to all. He was in trouble. Not booze or drug trouble, just stupid mouth and actions trouble, and the law. His parents had had it—he was booted out of the house with his step-father telling me not to take him in. John and I worked full-time. John was in his 70s with less patience than two decades ago. But we weren't going to throw him under the bus either.

Many of our days found us in court. A sentencing and ankle-lock time had arrived. Frank was a smart kid doing dumb things. If we could settle him down; get a routine in place; surround him with a new crowd … just maybe we'd pull him out. The court gave him permission to enroll in college. Getting him enrolled and gladly paying the tuition began the setting of a new stage for him. The court allowed him to travel back and forth—school to our home and back to school. He was tracked. Two years later, a different kid emerged and both John and I told ourselves that we were finished with parenting duties. We helped him move to his first apartment along with extra furniture that we had, and what he had gathered. He was excited; so were we and the rest of the family.

Life Is for the Living

A miracle is a celebration—a celebration of life. John used to hate holidays. He came from an unhappy home, an alcoholic mother, a non-caring family. He was always amazed at the festivities and the joy of planning that went into our holidays, whether it was Christmas or a birthday.

Frank's death fell on September 3, John's birthday. But it was also the first day of the Labor Day weekend. John needed his birthday back. We needed to celebrate life on his birthday, not death. We needed a miracle of resurrection. Now, to this day, I refer to Frank's death as being on Labor Day. John's birthday will always be on September 3. He is very much alive. John got his birthday back. I go out of my way to celebrate his day. Whether it's just us, or friends, it's his day. This is life continuing, always a miracle in my book.

Celebrating life in all its forms is one of my favorite pleasures, my greatest joys. I love to entertain, having friends over. Setting my table is one of life's simple pleasures; it's an art to me. It can be very simplistic or very ornate. A pot of geraniums. Mustard seeds. Whatever. Just so I'm celebrating life. When friends are over or I am hosting an event, it's a celebration acknowledging how important my friends are to me. I want them to know this when they are alive.

The older I get, the more I enjoy and appreciate life's simpler pleasures. You will never see me driving a Mercedes again. That wouldn't make me feel good about myself—surrounded by expensive toys for everyone else's benefit. For the first time in my life we had bought a used van. I was so tickled with us. We had broken the "need" to have the best, whatever one defines as the best. Instead, we have what we really need. Wheels that could haul stuff—mainly the many books that I routinely transport for speaking gigs.

As I pen this fourth expanded edition of *When God Says NO,* Frank is 31 and married, a celebration that was slated for the garden in my home and completed in my living room surrounded by friends when torrential rains flowed. He's joined by his younger brother and sister, Ryan and Bella who are in their teens. John is kissing 88 and I'm … well, I'm me, working full time with authors creating, strategizing and publishing books. It's now my purpose and I love it!

When you find yourself tempted, as Frank did when he was six years old, to say, "Life is too long, too hard and not fair." Stop … and take a moment to think about the powerful messages that are found in everyday life. And often the most powerful are the simplest.

The joys and sounds of holiday times fill the air with friends, family, music, and spirituality. I love the array of lights during Christmas time.

I look around me in awe when I first catch sight of the new green as leaves on trees in springtime promise to come forth.

I love the sun warming my face as I just sit down for quiet time on my deck.

I love the kiss of the morning air when I can feel fall is coming, along with sitting by my fireplace and reading, watching a movie, and being with friends.

I love the beauty of a gentle snow as it begins to dust the ground and the awesome landscape that promises to come.

And I love cooking and eating with friends. Open yourself to times with your friends. Spontaneous laughter with something you saw or heard. A wonderful meal … there is so much to live for and to love.

Today, I am rich with blessings. I have my health and I have my family. I have been rich. And I have been poor, very poor, as in welfare-type of poor. I have had great bouts of sickness, pain, disasters. Yet I am blessed. I have a good life. God reminds us that it's never hopeless. There's always, always—in the midst of heartache and tragedy—a blessing to remember, to find. A blessing to focus our minds on. A miracle … the miracle of life. Let's live it together and show the world what life is all about.

God doesn't send disasters our way. He does, though, send a miracle … a *yes* is that ability to cope with it; to grow from it. Once tragedy, disaster or misfortune strikes, use it as your personal eye-opening experience to learn, to stretch, to grow.

Life includes the gift of spirituality, finding solace and allowing it to envelop you. It's about becoming a little kid again—son Frank's final gift to me. And it's emerging from a cocoon and becoming a butterfly, a butterfly that is delighted with life and the discovery of its beauty. And it's about joy … that deep settled confidence that knowing you can trust again and can be in control. And last, it's knowing who you are.

Why am I so joyful? Because I've gone through so much.

That life has meaning and purpose … that there's a reason for your life. Your life will count for something more than just a momentary passage through this world. And your life holds the potential to touch others, to change them and add something good and positive in the continuum of this universe. You matter, infinitely, to those around you, to yourself.

As I close this book, my prayer for you is not that all your *whys* have been answered. They aren't going to be.

Rather, to move away from *why* and be ready for your *yes*. Somewhere, out there, it's ready to drop in. Look inside of yourself, view the future, your future, and find your reason to live, to be here.

Pain is inevitable … misery is not. This I believe.

Some of my speaker friends have queried me as to why I love life, why I love to laugh, why I always try to find the good side of any situation. The answer is simple. It's Frank's little kid/fun spirit he left with me. I'm willing to work enormously hard, put in long hours, but there's got to be fun. And that's part of the joy of life. I truly believe the amount of pain and agony I've experienced is directly parallel to the amount of joy I can feel and can give. One's cup of joy can only be as deep as one's sorrow.

Why am I so joyful? Because I've gone through so much. Will I have more negative experiences? Probably. But I have the tools: My sense of fun and knowledge of who I am and what I'm about, and that I have the resilience to overcome life's obstacles. *All my noes have led to yeses … even miracles.*

Since I was a little girl—over sixty years ago, I have been an avid reader of syndicated columns. When I was a kid, Ann Landers and Dear Abby were my go-to for "common sense" and "reality checks"—as millions did daily. For years, I clipped articles and tracked down books and poems that were cited. One column introduced me to the writings of Henry van Dyke. In his "A Parable of Immortality," he eloquently addresses the earthly departure of a loved one. I love his words.

> *I am standing upon the seashore. A ship at my side spreads her white sails to the morning breeze and starts for the ocean. She is an object of beauty and strength, and I watch until at last she hangs like a speck of white cloud just where the sun and sky come down to mingle. Then someone says, "There she goes!"*

> *Gone where? Gone from my sight—that is all. She is just as large in mast and hull and spar as she was when she left my side and just as able to bear her load of living freight to their destination.*

> *Her diminished size is in me, not in her. And just at the moment when someone at my side says, "There she goes!" other eyes watch her coming and other voices take up the shout, "Here she comes!"*

After Frank died, I felt horribly alone—deserted. Somehow, the 19 years he sailed with us were diminished. As if they never counted. There were times I felt that they were not experienced, rather a dream. It was years before I embraced and relished that I had 19 years of memories, with some as huge as a white mast, while others a mere speck on the horizon.

But they were memories … our memories … goofy memories; fun memories; loving memories; regretful memories; and memories of when I wanted to kick him in the butt. My memories … and no one can withhold them. What a gift to receive.

You and everyone you know will experience rough times. No one has an exclusive on good times, a perfect or charmed life. Each of us will undergo *noes,* some of us, a lot. When they occur, stop. You don't have the luxury to get stuck on *why.* Why begets more whys. Stop.

Many of the awful times in my life have been created by things and others that I couldn't control. To me, forgiveness is not about letting someone off the hook for wrongdoings —legally, ethically, morally. Real forgiveness has a different meaning for me. I can forgive myself for being vulnerable;

for being naïve; for screwing up … so I can let myself off the hook.

Get ready to move on. To be ready for the *yes* that is coming your way. *Here it comes!*

You are a gift. A miracle. And I'm thankful you have come into my life at this time.

CHAPTER SIXTEEN

Hello Big Sky Country

We were minimalists before we'd ever heard
the word or knew what it was.

It was 1963 ... and I was all of sixteen years old. And, I was leaving California for the Big Sky Country: Montana! I was excited; my first real adventure to another state. A new environment ... a new life, and the new life within me, awaited me. I was married and pregnant.

Graduating from high school at 16, there wasn't much a 16-year-old could do back in the early '60s to support herself. Staying "home" wasn't an option, not for me. What were my options? Not the military or being an airline stewardess; I was 16. Not college—the financial support that was planned for my brothers wasn't available for me.

After all, I was just a girl. I had a part-time job that paid $1.00 an hour and babysitting was 50 cents an hour. Or, I could get married. And I did—escaping from my home.

Steve had been accepted at Montana State University and tuition was covered. We left Los Angeles and headed to our destination 1,100 miles away—Bozeman, Montana.

As my pregnancy advanced, I got a phone call from a nurse. My doctor had given my name to the nursing school that he had a "young, pregnant" patient who would welcome a nursing student to help her. Surprised, I invited her over; what did I have to lose? I was so ignorant about birthing and infant care, anything would be good.

Julia was wonderful. She had always wanted to be a nurse, and she was a mom, too. At 30, she'd enrolled at the college to earn her RN. She checked in with me weekly, explaining what would be happening to my changing body as it prepped for the eventual birth, even showing up with photos and diagrams and diapers! I practiced diapering and was told the best way to wash them. Remember, this is the '60s—no disposables. I washed everything … and I mean everything, by hand,

There's a little problem with her feet.

and hung laundry on an outside line. This was quite an incentive for early potty training!

My time was coming and on a snowy Tuesday morning, calls went out to my doctor and Julia. Labor had started and the doctor wanted me to be at his office when it opened. As he examined me, he promised it was going to be a long day—most likely the baby would not be here until evening. I was to stay in touch throughout the day with his office. His nurse suggested we go to a movie, which we did for $1 for the two of us.

"It's a perfect little girl," Julia said as my daughter debuted that night, two weeks before her due date. Tired, I vaguely heard the doctor say, "There's a little problem with her feet." I didn't know what that meant.

I loved everything about the birthing experience. No drugs. All natural. I had done my part; the doctor had done his. Baby Briles had been taken to the nursery. I would be taken to the maternity "ward" for a four-day stay. But Julia was not ready for me to be moved just yet. Julia told the ward nurse, "In a few minutes … I'll bring her over … I've one more thing to do here."

That one more thing was the best! She proceeded to give me a wonderful table bath and freshened me up for my night's sleep. Silly me, I thought having a bath in the delivery room was normal; all new moms got this treatment. Wrong. When Frank was born 15 months later, there was no Julia or any nurse like her, and definitely no "cleanup" bath. What was I thinking? When I think of her decades later, it always brings fond memories and a smile to my face. How incredibly fortunate my baby and I were to have had Julia in our lives.

Those were the days before the concept of "rooming in" was introduced, at least in Montana. Those were the days where moms and babies stayed anywhere from three to five days in the hospital and the nurses would stay with new, inexperienced moms as we learned how to nurse our babies. Schedules? Nope! Newborns were kept in the nursery and brought to the mom when baby started the "I'm hungry" cry. And the cost of my hospital stay in 1963? It was a huge amount to us: $90. We paid off the bill over six months!

On Shelley's first checkup, I learned what the "feet" problem was called—club feet. Her legs and feet were extremely twisted inward. Adding that it could improve, our family doctor said, "We may have to take corrective measures," whatever that meant.

The doctor had given me some manipulations to do on her feet. "Just a few minutes a day," he said. Shelley was already glued to my arms. Even when she slept, I often just held her, amazed at this marvel that had come from my body. "I will take care of you, little one" became my lullaby to her. I'd quickly decided that those few minutes could easily be repeated multiple times a day. So, throughout the day, my hands were automatically on her little feet, gently turning them. Shelley and I spent hours together in the rocking chair that I bought for $2 at a yard sale along with a TV for $3 that sat on top of a Radio Flyer red wagon I found in a trash pickup.

At four months, both her legs were enveloped in full casts that were replaced with new ones as she grew that first year. I was sensitive to the looks people would give me as her leg casts poked out under whatever she was wearing.

I will take care of you, little one.

People would ask me, "What happened to her?" Or, "How did she get hurt?"

When the casts came off at year-end, she and I started up again on the feet exercises as she sat in my lap—a lap that was now bulging with another baby on the way. Within a few months, her feet were braced when she went to bed. I hated putting them on her. I'll never forget the time I went in her room in the middle of the night and she said, "Mommy, take these damn braces off!" Instead, I sat on the floor by her bed stroking her forehead as she fell back to sleep.

The date we could officially stop using the "Denis Brown brace" was huge for her … and from two years of age on, Shelley's feet looked and worked like other kids. No one would know that she'd had clubbed feet. We fixed them!

We were minimalists before we'd ever heard the word or knew what it was. The difference is that we hadn't chosen to be minimalists. We were flat broke, living on $150 a month with most of the money going toward rent and utilities. We budgeted $10 a month for food and another $5 for miscel-

> I failed at it. I would give all critters a head start.

laneous. We didn't know that there were aid programs— we just made do, kind of. Potatoes and instant milk were staples for us.

That, plus the "poaching" we did. Yup, Steve hunted and had dead deer hanging in a garage next door to our basement apartment. He decided I needed to learn how to hunt. I failed at it. I would give all critters a head start. My job then became the cleaner. I gagged when I did it. To this day, I can't look at venison.

Sometimes, we would go down to the local grocery store and covet the food in front of us. We were so hungry at times that I even stole food from Buttrey's Supermarkets. Years later, I sent a check for $200 with a letter telling the president what I had done and apologized. My check was returned with a letter thanking me for reaching out and asking me to send a new check to someone else in need or a cause I cared about. I gladly did, sending it to Planned Parenthood.

Simply Montana

When Shelley arrived, it was deep winter. Frank arrived in early summer the next year—a time in Montana that is simply sensational, along with the trout fishing.

One afternoon, our mailman stopped to talk with me while I was hanging out the wash. He pointed out that he lived up the street from us and that he had a baby boy who might be the same age as Shelley. He was heading home to have lunch and encouraged me to come up and meet his wife and little Tommy. We did and Faye came into my life.

The gardens I planted flourished under the sunny days with seeds that she generously shared. She showed me about the wonders of canning our harvests and the secret to trout fishing: yellow and green miniature marshmallows when worms weren't available. We baked together weekly, experimenting with different cookie recipes. Snickerdoodles became a favorite.

When I realized that I was pregnant again, she promised to give me all of Tommy's outgrown clothes if I had a boy. Back then there was no way to learn a baby's gender in utero. The reveal party happened at delivery time.

Shelley and Tommy became fast friends and spent a lot of time together as we moms drank tea and baked. During the winter months, our mobility was limited. As spring came and then summer, Faye and I spent much of our time outdoors gardening and enjoying the weather. One afternoon, the two of us were standing outside by the curb in front of my apartment. We both heard

My friend saved one, possibly two lives.

a motorcycle coming down the street. Turning toward the noise, Faye immediately jumped in front of me as the bike leaped over the curb—taking a direct hit to her body.

My friend was down. I was eight months pregnant and stood intact, but extremely shaken by what had just happened. The motorcycle guy got up and moved toward Faye. I ran to my neighbor to get help and call for an ambulance.

Leaving Shelley and Tommy with my neighbor, I went with Faye. Her arm and pelvis were broken. The doctors said that if I had taken the hit, my baby would have died, and I would have been critically hurt. We never knew what happened to the motorcycle guy. What I did know was that my friend saved one, possibly two lives.

Faye was out of the hospital and healing. And baby Frank arrived the next week, three weeks early. I was sure the stress of what had happened had hastened his arrival. Shortly thereafter, her husband got a new route and they moved across town, a ten-minute drive.

Steve had gotten a summer job driving for Coca Cola, so I had the use of the car. One morning, I headed to Faye's as we girls needed a cookie baking session and her new backyard was loaded with red worms, perfect for fishing. Plus, as promised, I garnered a bunch of little boy clothes. Frank was now three months old and Shelley was 18 months old.

After several hours of our little ones playing, cookie baking and finally worm digging, Faye and I were talking by the car, saying our good-byes with Shelley and Tommy at our feet and a baby in my arms, along with a coffee can of worms. First, I put the worms on the car top so I could place Frank on the passenger side floor, cushioned by towels so he wouldn't roll around. Reaching for Shelley, I added her to the passenger seat. Immediately, she stood up. No matter, I have a Mommy Arm to take care of her. The Mommy Arm was the precursor of the car seat and to this day, I unconsciously fling it out if another is in the car with me and I must do a sudden stop when driving.

When I got home, the phone was ringing. Faye was on the other end. "Missing something?" she asked.

"I don't think so." Then I remembered the worms. I'd forgotten to take them off the roof of the car before I drove off. So "yes," the can of worms was missing.

"Anything else?" she asked. Puzzled, I looked around and then saw the anything else!

I took home the wrong child! I took her Tommy—same size, same hair color and length, same jibber-jabber as my Shelley. And Tommy had talked to me all the way home, while I held my arm across his little body, keeping my eyes on the road. Geez!

We both laughed hysterically. Back I went for the kid exchange.

Fast Forward

Montana is now 50 plus years ago. In 2016, John and I moved from our Colorado home of 20 years—a downsizing of yard maintenance and an easier living style. John is almost 16 years older than I am and dealing with a variety of physical challenges that aging brings. I needed a home that I could do most of the maintenance on, no longer relying on him. With the big move, I put together a memory box for each daughter and wrapped them as Christmas gifts, telling them to do with as they chose. I had saved hospital birth records, report cards, drawings, photos, etc. Stuff I had squirreled away over the past 50 years.

They had the best time going through their memory boxes, giggling at what was contained in each. I had kept Shelley's hospital bill when she was born and the bill for her tonsil's surgery—why I kept the bill for tonsils, I'm clueless. What a hoot. Hospital bills! I even saved the hospital bill for Frank, just 15 months after Shelley was born. It had jumped significantly … to $120.

By the time I was 20, I was the mother of three with Sheryl joining Shelley and Frank. Although I was very young, oh-so-naïve, poor, and not knowing any better, I am thankful to this day that I had them early. Each of my babies was such a miracle to me, it's no wonder that I held onto each long after she or he fell asleep. With each baby, I knew I held perfection in my arms.

Motherhood. A huge YES!

CHAPTER SEVENTEEN

My Final Thoughts ...
the Gift of Resiliency

For me, my life is like a rose ...
wonderful fragrances ...
spectacular colors and shapes ...
and a few horrendous thorns.

Yes, pain is inevitable, misery is not. I know of no one that
I have met who hasn't had curveballs thrown at them. Bad
times do happen; sometimes they feel and look like an
avalanche that is never ending. The potholes of life deliver
choices that must be made. You can choose to sink and
drown or learn to swim.

My choice is to swim, fully aware that there will be more
potholes down the road. I tell my audiences that the person
I am today is not the result of the successes that I have

had … and there have been plenty … but the result of the disasters, failures, mistakes, and pain that I have endured and grown from. And, there have been plenty … strength through adversity. Yeses from noes.

Re-dealing My Deck

People who are close to me know that I often say, "God gave me the wrong deck …." Somehow, I knew that I was being raised in a family … my birth family … who didn't want me and didn't like me. I was basically invisible. I have no memory of my birth mother until after I was seven. I do have a clear memory of Lotti—a housekeeper who loved to watch the horse races on a very small black and white TV (this is the early '50s) and who took me home with her occasionally. She became a little girl's ally. Other females in our house were nonexistent.

My early childhood has lots of blanks. I have memories of my brothers stoning me as I ran across a field; of my father carrying me into an ER to sew my head up; of my brothers pushing me into a pool; of watching TV with Lotti—our housekeeper who was my friend and would take me home sometimes on weekends; of the big earthquake in Los

Angeles where we lived in 1952; and firetrucks coming to our house. Memories before the age of seven.

My birth mother's existence is a complete blank. Her visibility surfaced when my father moved all four of us kids to a beach town in Southern California that I loved for so many reasons. And most likely, the magnet generator that water and sun have for me to this day. Our move was spawned by a situation. My five-year-old brother had burned down part of the house we lived in by setting off some fireworks in the garage.

I came alive at the beach. It woke up my fun factor. I also discovered my first Heart Family. It was a family with four girls and it was a tribe I wanted to be part of. And I happily wagered every sleeping and waking moment to stay with them ... and I lucked out! "Uncle Dave" gave me my first set of wheels—a used bicycle that he painted and allowed me to travel up and down the beach strand with ease, pulling a red wagon I found. With that wagon, I became a gatherer of empty bottles. I took the bottles to what was called the Green Store on Sundays. In return, I got two cents for each soda bottle and five cents for each beer bottle. It became my "treat" money—fifty cents took me to the movies all day, along with popcorn and a soda.

I overheard "Aunt Nina" say to him, "Her family is weird," not knowing what that meant. The word "weird" wasn't in my vocabulary. And to me, "I'll teach you how to play cards and sew and you can stay here any time you want." And she did and I did.

I was transported to what a family who cared for themselves and for others was all about—where a young girl could start to grow up. But after five years, it abruptly changed. My birth family moved—something to do with my older brother needing to get away from the ocean because of asthma. They made me go with them. I was devastated and lost once again. Enrolled in my new school, I met Linda Briles. Another deck of cards was dealt, and a new world opened, which would impact me for the rest of my life and eventually bring my own children into my life.

She became the icing on my growing-up cake.

The Briles' world created a whirlwind of activity. Something I craved. Linda's mother became my true Heart Mother. Everything about Joyce Briles I adored, and I took in. She was kind and caring. She loved me. Taking me under her wing, she became the icing on my growing-up cake. She

was my role model for housekeeping to parenting to enter-
taining. And it was Joyce who opened the door of courage.
In her mid-forties, the mother of six filed for divorce. I
looked in the mirror and said to myself ... *This is you. Do
you want to go through it at 46 or 26?* I opted for 26. When
I told her, she held me and said, "I'm so sorry—this will be
hard on you."

Little did I know how hard it would be as I started the
extraction from her eldest son, the man I had dated and
married ten years prior. When she got the news that Frank
had fallen to his death, she was on the next plane to be
with me.

My Epiphany

The only hint that my ultimate vocation would become
writing and speaking first emerged in third grade. I got
in trouble at school. In fact, I was in trouble a lot. You see,
I talked too much. And I passed notes to my friends in
class. Teachers didn't like that; I thought it was normal.

It wasn't until decades later when I was the president of a
college foundation in Northern California that real writing
became the gleam in my eye ... a book. Of course, it was

to be just one book. But it didn't start out as a book idea; it started out as a dinner.

As the president of the foundation, there were perks. One was that I was always included in the private dinners held for our guest lecturers. One evening our speaker was my dinner companion. We had a lovely time. We laughed and commiserated about each having teenagers—getting parents together when each has three teens is sure to pepper the conversation. I had shared a discussion that I had had with Frank of what the draft was like before it ended.

Then, my mind took a side-trip … it started with a "what if …." What if we took away driving for two years instead of having a draft? Think about it: Accidents would decline; auto insurance rates would drop; parents would save money; school grades would increase; and the list went on.

He used my ideas and got paid for them.

Little did I know that he was actively listening, chalking up a slew of ideas that he would turn into a column based on things I had said during the three hours we were together.

A week later when I was in Mexico on a business trip, picking up the morning's edition of the *Los Angeles Times,* I discovered his column—filled with all my ideas around raising teenagers. Oh, the column was amusing, but I wasn't feeling so amused. In fact, I was ticked. He never even told me he was thinking of writing about our conversation, let alone asking for my permission. Upon my return, there was a letter thanking me for the evening and telling me (warning me?) that he might use some of "our" ideas in a future column.

It was signed, *Cheers—Art Buchwald.*

Future? How about past tense? What the heck ... he used my ideas and got paid for them.

Yet, the "aha" dropped in—my epiphany. All that ran through my mind was, "If I don't start taking some of my own ideas, others will take them ... and make money." That was April of 1979. Eight months later, I had sold my first book.

I wrote too many notes in school and got caught; I talked too much and was sent home multiple times because I couldn't keep still or quiet. I didn't follow all the rules.

Who would have known that they were precursors to my livelihood: being an author and being a professional speaker? Sometimes you don't know what seeds an idea. Who would have known that someone taking my ideas and using them would in turn seed a profession that I love? And one that wasn't on my radar!

A Speech, High Tea, and the Unexpected

In the mid-2000s, I was looking forward to checking off one of the items on my personal bucket list—having High Tea in Victoria, Canada, and strolling through the sensational Butchart Gardens. John and I had made our reservations to celebrate our final day in Canada with a day trip to Victoria. Finishing my last presentation at a huge dental conference in British Columbia, we headed to the final dinner for all attendees in the ballroom. I didn't get far. Within minutes, I was flat on my back, stunned that I was no longer walking. Rattled, I struggled to get up, wondering, *what …?*

I couldn't get up on my own. Guests in the lobby rushed to help John get me upright. "There's white stuff all over you," he said. "What happened?"

"I don't know, but there is wet stuff all over the floor ..."
I answered.

What we learned months later was that the "white stuff"
was ice cream or yogurt, dropped on the floor by a guest.
My foot found it on the hotel lobby's white marble floor.
We went on to the dinner, walking slowly as my body hurt. I
realized that I couldn't stay and headed back to our room.

It was a rough night. Silently, I was beginning to think
I had broken my hip as I attempted to get up the next
morning. But, by golly, I was going to High Tea and see
the gardens, so I told John I was fine.

It was not good. I kept falling asleep on the ride to our
destination. I could barely walk in the gardens and the
thought of a wheel chair was sounding good to me. John
used a cane at that time, and I asked him if he would mind
sharing. Cutting short our visit, we headed to the hotel
that was hosting the High Tea. Sitting down, our server
approached us and suggested champagne, in addition to
the tea selection. I don't remember the tea ... I do remember guzzling down several glasses of the alternative—
self-medication to numb the pain in my body.

Everything became foggy. We made it back to Colorado the next day. My fogginess stayed with me and friends dropped by to see how I was. John opened a bottle of wine; I took a sip … and spit it out. Everyone was as surprised as I was. The taste was awful. Enjoying a glass of wine was something that I usually loved to enjoy with dinner and socially with friends.

A few days later, I was talking to a friend, and she noticed that I was slurring a few words … or forgetting them. She suggested that I see a doctor.

Oh-oh … I needed some serious help … it was time to reach out to the medical community. I could barely read for almost 18 months; I lost my ability to do math. And I couldn't handle multiple voices around me. It was like everyone was yelling at me at the same time. Food tasted different … or I couldn't tolerate certain ones anymore. For some time, I couldn't even tie a bow.

I was a mess, and everything seemed out of control. The fear that my mind was turning to mush loomed in front of me. How could this be happening? Help was needed— a lot of it. Neurologists, chiropractors, ophthalmologists, surgeons, physical therapy, eye therapy and pain management took over my life for the next two years.

My fall had delivered a brain injury and body injuries—the unexpected. Everything seemed like a huge NO around me.

With multiple surgeries, almost a dozen hospitalizations for pain management and extensive physical therapy, my body was moving again and working better. With the eye therapy and the guidance and encouragement of Dr. Lynn Hellerstein, I could once again do what I loved: read. Not at the speed-reading levels I did in the past, but ahead of the average level of most. Some foods along with alcohol and sodas were no longer in my diet. And, my head was getting better—it no longer felt like mush.

During this time, John began to travel with me to meet my speaking contract commitments. I was fully booked out for a year and wasn't capable of handling it all. He watched over me; made sure I got to the stage I would speak from; handled all our book sales ... and got me back to my hotel room so my fired-up brain could calm down ... and sleep. Then John got me to my next gig.

I knew that I could no longer deal with the road travel that my work required—at its peak, speaking took me to a dozen states within one month. My new meds and my body wouldn't tolerate the travel required. What was I going to do to make a living … for the rest of my life?

The answer—the gift of "yes"—was in front of me. Since the publication of my first book in 1981, I have always had a "pay it forward" philosophy when it came to publishing and wannabe authors. An author friend had sat down with me three months before my first book launched and guided me through what to expect and what I needed to do to support my book. The two hours she spent with me morphed my attitude about what was needed for achieving authordom—which seeded the success of that first book, *The Woman's Guide to Financial Savvy* with St. Martin's Press.

I was willing to help anyone who was interested in publishing. My knowledge brought me full circle to publishing as my next adventure … with books … with authors. With my fall, I lost my rapid ability to do math. But with this loss, I discovered an ability to "see books" … when authors talked to me about their books and showed me their manuscripts, I began to "see" what they should look like … how they should be laid out and presented to the reader. This was now my new business and I am thriving.

Ever since I can remember, I have loved books—the look, the touch, the smell, and what lies between the covers. My "yes" was to professionally do what I had been doing personally for 30 years ... helping other authors do what I do with writing and publishing my books. Thus, The Book Shepherd was born. People come to me to create, strategize, write, develop, publish, and market their books. The immense joy I feel when a new book—a new baby—is conceived, birthed, and published is priceless. And the bonus: My travel dropped 90 percent.

One last word ...

Since its first publication in 1990, *When God Says NO* has enjoyed multiple editions and printings. I have had letters, emails and phone calls from friends and been approached by strangers wanting and needing to reach out ... to connect. To be assured that there is hope within their sea of hurt: of dealing with trauma; of dealing with disasters; of dealing with misfortune; of dealing with death; and of dealing with life.

I so get it ... I was, and am, one of them ... one of you.

The wrong things; the wrong times; even the wrong people are all too common. Today's violence, the disintegration of family life and families, the uproar in politics, and the bombarding negativity only reinforce the desire for one to exit, stage right.

Don't. You count, tremendously. You have seen that I have traveled many paths; some of them extremely painful—mentally, spiritually, physically, even materially. I know you have, too. You do not fail because of the mistakes or disasters exposed by the path you are on. You don't fail because of setbacks along your path.

You set yourself up for failure when you choose not to get back up when a situation knocks you down. You only fail when you quit shuffling; a better deck will come your way. Keep shuffling.

For years I wondered why I wasn't a fit with my birth family. I even wondered if I had been adopted and said so to my younger brother. I mean, I wasn't like my birth parents. But I wasn't. Many years later, my old brother stumbled across an uncle—my mother's brother—who revealed more of the family history. They didn't know about we four kids from my parents, as we didn't know about them.

I never had grandparents in my life ... how could I, they didn't know I, or my brothers, existed.

Whatever went on in that family, there was a brick wall between females—somehow, they all disliked each other. When I came along, I was the spitting image of my grandmother per the photos that the uncle shared with my brother. To me, it explained why my birth mother wanted nothing to do with me—I looked like her mother! Her lack of female friends lends me to believe that she just didn't like other women ... or little girls.

When my kids were in their early teens, my eldest daughter said, "You need to be like a Gramma to our cousins ... your mother doesn't like girls." Her sister echoed the same thing—wise ones, my girls are.

My YES was that I did find a Heart Mother who did like little girls ... in fact, I had two of them.

In my early seventies now, I can say that some decades I would never want to repeat; others have been rich and thrilling. For me, my life is like a rose ... wonderful fragrances ... spectacular colors and shapes ... and a few horrendous thorns. Living with and through those thorns has woven the fabric of who I am today.

Many times, I've landed in a "sink or swim" scenario ...
but first, I had to learn how to tread water. The *fourth gift
of resiliency* was always with me, I just didn't recognize it
or know what to call it. It was, and is, the gift that keeps on
giving. For that, I am thankful.

For whatever reason you have this book in your hands, in
your thoughts, and in your heart, there is a reason. We are
in this together. There is a YES.

Judith

In Gratitude ...

This book has been in my heart for many years. It took me five years after Frank died before I could sit down and start writing. The first edition was published in 1990 with updated editions in 1994 and 1997.

The later editions were quickly tweaked and then republished. Although I rarely spoke on the book or the topic, it was a book that sold thousands and thousands of copies. It was a book that I would tell close friends "had legs" ... routinely, my display copy would just disappear from the table where it was for sale with my other books at conferences where I spoke. Whiff ... just disappear. I let it go, believing that whoever had taken it needed it.

When God Says NO has been introspective for me. My friends, family, and buyers of it have been overwhelmed by its message. The letters and calls that I have received from recipients have been too numerous to even try to keep count of. Many have bought the book for friends who are in pain.

The calls and emails are coming in once again: Won't you republish *When God Says NO*? And now, twenty-plus years since the last edition, it is time once again to reread and write. Little did I know that a total re-write would roll out, revealing so much more about my life and the obstacles encountered and overcome.

Friends and family asked me: Do you really want to write about such a painful time in your life again? Do you want to reveal some of your failures, your mistakes, and expose yourself to old hurts and wounds? Many wounds that had already healed?

The answer was yes. I could do it again. As I settled in to write about my sons and other significant events of my past, I learned a lot about myself. Reflection was in play. I had healed, I had grown, and I could reach out and give to others, with no expectations in return.

Thank you to my immediate family: John, Shelley, Sheryl, Frank, Ryan and Bella. Without their encouragement and support, my journey in bringing it to you would have been extremely difficult.

To Joyce Briles, my Heart Mother, who became my role model for living and dropped everything to be at my side during my darkest hours.

To my "Heart Sisters" Ellen Tryon and Glenda Squire, always with me in spirit and when needed, in person.

To Marilyn Van Derbur Atler, a voice for millions and one of the many voices of encouragement who supported this new edition.

To Deb Sheppard, who helps so many through their grief. Her push was a motivator for years to get "my story" out ... all 50 shades of the purple I've traveled and grown through.

To Jean Hollands, Alan Leavens, and Reverend John Snyder who were there unconditionally when it seemed the darkest. And to new guides including Rabbi Joseph Schultz whose wisdom flows by my side.

To Rebecca Finkel, who is the visionary of covers and interior designs for countless books.

To Peggie Ireland, Barb Wilson, Pat Morgan, Leah DaSalla, and Sandy Lawrence for editing, insight and professional support.

You all are a gift to me, a YES.

About the Author

Judith Briles is known as The Book Shepherd and an encourager. She is a Speaker, Author and Publishing expert, Radio Host, and the Founder and Chief Visionary Officer of AuthorYOU.org.

As the author of 37 books, she has earned over 30 national book awards in the Writing, Publishing and Business categories from the International Book Awards, USA Best Book Awards, National Indie Excellence Awards, IPPY Awards, Parents' Choice Awards, Foreword INDIES Book of the Year, Independent Press Award, Book Excellence Awards,

CIPA Evvy Awards, Colorado Center for the Book Award and Global eBook Awards. In 2017, she was honored to be awarded the first Dan Poynter Legacy Award in Nonfiction.

In 2000, she created Mile High Press after publishing 18 books with New York houses. Based in Colorado, she's published in 16 countries with more than 1,000,000 copies of her work sold. All books in the *AuthorYOU Mini-Guide Series* have earned #1 Best Seller status on Amazon.

Calling Colorado her home base, she marvels at the human spirit in its quest to survive and thrive.

Connect with her at:

TheBookShepherd.com
Judith@Briles.com

And Follow her on:

 @MyBookShepherd @JudithBriles

 Judith Briles-The Book Shepherd

 JudithBriles

 Judith.TheBookShepherd

Judith Briles
Consults and Speaks

Would You Like to Listen ...
Learn ... Publish?

Judith Briles would be delighted to participate in your publishing conference or to speak to your group. For Book Shepherding and Book Consulting, email or call her offices.

If you want a highly interactive, informative and fun presentation or workshop, call or email her for availability.

Workshops and Keynotes include:

If Publishing Is in Your Midst ...
  Which Option Is for YOU and YOUR Book?

Is There a Book in You?

How to Create Your Author and Book Platforms

Creating Confidence as an Author & Writer

Creating Confidence when Adversity is at
  Your Doorstep

The Art of Ninja Book Marketing

Pitch YOU in 15 Seconds or Less

Avoid the Blunders, Bloopers, and Boo-Boos That Can Sink Your Book

Craft a Talk That Sells Thousands of Books and Can Make Over $1,000,000

Attend the Judith Briles Unplugged events:
Book Publishing and Speaking
Details and dates are on her website, www.Briles.com under "Events".

Coaching and Consulting:
By the hour or for a book project. In addition, Judith has private one-on-one coaching online (or by phone), or within a group.

If you want publishing information and resources to help you sell books.
Discover blogs: Radio shows that are available in podcasting format and social media accounts, all designed to deliver information for today's author.

All Events are posted on Judith's website:

www.TheBookShepherd.com

Judith@Briles.com • 303-885-2207